JAMES MCENANEY is a jo[...]r
secondary school teache[...]
Scottish education, having [...]
schools for publications in [...]es,
The Herald, The Sunday Na[...]u many more.
He has contributed chapter[...] anthologies – *A Nation
Changed? The SNP and Scotland Ten Years On* and *Scotland
the Brave? Twenty Years of Change and the Future of the Nation*
– and is the author of *A Scottish Journey: Personal Impressions
of Modern Scotland*.

Class Rules
The Truth About Scottish Schools

JAMES MCENANEY

Luath Press Limited
EDINBURGH
www.luath.co.uk

First published 2021

ISBN: 978-1-910022-60-3

The author's right to be identified as author of this book
under the Copyright, Designs and Patents Act 1988 has been asserted.

The paper used in this book is recyclable. It is made
from low chlorine pulps produced in a low energy,
low emissions manner from renewable forests.

MIX
Paper from
responsible sources
FSC® C022174

Printed and bound by
Severnprint Ltd, Gloucester

Typeset in 10.5 point Sabon by
Main Point Books, Edinburgh

Contents

Contents

For Ruth and Ciaran, still the most important people in Scotland, and for all of those who believe in a better future.

Introduction

WHEN THE FIRST coronavirus lockdown began in March 2020, a book on Scottish schooling – the idea for which had been brewing for months – was going to be my great personal achievement. While some people were learning languages, nurturing sourdough starters or finally getting the loft organised, I would be pulling together all my work from the past few years, and maybe adding some contributions from a range of others across the education system, in order to finally do what no one else would: tell people the truth about Scottish schools.

But it turns out that living through a deadly global pandemic isn't particularly conducive to high levels of concentration, productivity or self-belief; 2020 came and went without a single word committed to a page, as did the first few months of 2021.

And then, on the ninth of March, I received the following email out of the blue from Gavin MacDougall of Luath Press, publisher of my first book, *A Scottish Journey*:

> Would you be interested in writing/compiling a book on the future of education in Scotland? If so, happy to arrange a time for a phone call to discuss.
>
> Best wishes,
> Gavin

A frantic fortnight later, with an outline submitted and a rough publication date established, I had agreed to finally write the book that I had been thinking about for nearly two years. The idea behind it hasn't really changed. Over the course of the coming chapters I am going to help you cut through the endless political grandstanding, media misrepresentations, impenetrable statistical releases and pernicious class-based assumptions that obscure so much of Scottish education and, with it, the reality of our society as a whole.

Put simply: I am indeed going to tell you the truth about Scottish schools.

But before we get to that, I should probably let you know exactly where I'm coming from. Back in 2010, a couple of years after leaving university with an English degree and no plans whatsoever, I reluctantly applied to become a teacher. By the time I got around to it, however, the deadline had long since passed, and I was relieved to discover that courses at both Strathclyde and Glasgow universities were already full – but then the University of the West of Scotland invited me for an interview and, soon after, offered me a place. A few weeks later, I was a student teacher; a year after that, I was preparing my first lessons in my own classroom.

In Scotland, new teachers are offered one year of guaranteed work as part of the national induction scheme. Most soon-to-qualify teachers apply to the programme and rank their top five preferences of local authorities in which to be placed, but there is another option: you can *tick the box*. Doing so means that you agree to be sent to any part of the country – it could be somewhere you've never been or a school five minutes from your house – but in exchange you receive an extra £6,000 if you're a primary teacher and £8,000 if you work in a secondary school.

I had recently gotten engaged and thought an extra eight grand sounded like a fantastic idea, so I *ticked the box*, took the cash, and was sent to teach at Arran High School, a job that I am utterly convinced will forever be the best I ever had. I was incredibly lucky to find myself in an English department run by Alan Kelly, a brilliant and hugely experienced teacher who has probably had more of an impact on my adult life than anyone else outside of my family. When I met him, I was 24 years old, excited and eager but a bit daunted nonetheless. On my first day, he sat me down in my new classroom and asked me, straight up, can you teach?

'Yeah... I think so.'

'Good.'

He told me that working in such a small school – we made up two thirds of the entire English staff – and in his department meant that, if I was up for it, I'd be allowed to get on with the job, and I'd have as much support as possible to get really good at it. That was true for every single minute of the two years for which I was lucky enough to work with Alan before he took a well-earned retirement, and remained the case under his replacement.

At the end of my first year at the school I secured the English teacher job on a permanent basis. My wife and I were married that summer, and we moved into a little terraced house that looked out onto the fields and hills behind Lamlash. We got a dog, a border collie that I trained on the beach every day, and near the end of my third year on the island (our second together) we had a son. I loved those years on Arran. I had every intention of staying for a very long time and giving my boy a very different childhood from my own – but sometimes life gets in the way. In the end, circumstances largely revolving around healthcare, transport, and the general antipathy with which the central belt treats life on the islands meant that my family and I reluctantly returned to the mainland in October 2014.

Since then, I have been a college lecturer. I deliver a variety of 'communication' units to students in a range of different courses, but also teach National 5 and Higher English to people who have, for whatever reason, left school without them. It has been a privilege to help those looking for a second chance in education, although I have lost track of the number who should never have *needed* to be in my class in the first place: those who have only been forced to spend additional years attaining these qualifications in a college – sometimes at significant short-term and long-term expense – because they were failed by a school system designed for the benefit of others.

But in recent years something else has happened. Quite by accident I have drifted back towards an earlier, thus far frustrated, ambition: journalism.

It began with regular comment pieces on *CommonSpace*, a new media platform established by the Common Weal think tank following the 2014 independence referendum. Then in 2015, one of my first forays into Freedom of Information (FOI) requests turned into a year-long battle with the Scottish Government to uncover the truth about their standardised testing programme. In the end I revealed that the policy didn't come out of any sort of detailed consultation – in fact, the government's total written advice on the issue amounted to just four unsolicited emails from two individuals. Winning that fight, and publishing information that the government had been desperate to keep secret from the public, ended up being just the start.

After that, either alone or alongside the likes of Andrew Denholm (then of *The Herald*), Rob Edwards (*The Ferret*) or Severin Carrell (*The Guardian*), and very often supported by *CommonSpace* editor Angela Haggerty, I continued to investigate a range of issues in Scottish education. I learned to combine my knowledge of the system with the various complexities of FOI legislation to break stories like the narrowing options for pupils in poorer areas of Scotland, the lack of libraries in schools across the country, or even Prince Charles' secret lobbying of the Scottish Government on behalf of Teach First, a fast-track teacher training provider from England. I also began to analyse and explain existing public data such as annual exam results and literacy rates, and in 2020 both predicted and then helped to break the story of the Scottish Qualifications Authority (SQA) results scandal.

Through all this time I had become increasingly frustrated by the fact that so much of the story of our schools remains inaccessible to many people, making it impossible for the public to know what is really going on and, as a consequence, undermining both faith in the system and our ability to hold our leaders to account.

Every single person in Scotland has some kind of stake in the effectiveness of the nation's schools, so in writing this book my goal was to explain the intricacies and inconsistencies of the system, and to explore its strengths and weaknesses, in a way that would make sense to as many people as possible. I am not attempting to map the entire landscape of the Scottish education system, nor provide all the answers for how to make things better; instead, my focus has been on the issues that dominate the national debate over schooling – such as the 'attainment gap', teacher numbers or the problems with Curriculum for Excellence – and the changes that could make the biggest difference to young people's experiences in the classroom.

Every chapter that follows, and even a number of the sub-chapters, could and probably should be whole books in their own right. There are times when I have had to sacrifice a bit of depth in exchange for much-needed clarity, which inevitably means that certain features, problems and controversies have been dealt with only briefly, while others have not been included at all. The physical state of Scotland's schools, the ongoing debate surrounding the inclusion agenda and the role of religion in our education system are just three of a range of important issues that I have, at least on this occasion, been unable to explore.

While putting these pages together I found myself examining a system that may not quite be collapsing, but which is certainly under enormous and unsustainable strain. One where both teachers and pupils are too often the victims of a compromised curriculum, insufficient support, unreliable and even misleading data, poor-quality journalism and commentary, a dearth of serious leadership, the weight of an imagined past, the pressure of impossible expectations, the grip of small-c conservatism, and politicians' willingness to weaponise our kids for their own benefit. In short, we have a school system that is both in need of and ripe for radical – even revolutionary – reform.

But it goes further than that. I have spent the last six years investigating and analysing the challenges facing Scottish education, immersing myself in official data and even helping to expand its scope – but had never brought all of it together before now. I always knew that the various problems affecting the system were endlessly interconnected, and that social inequality is ultimately the main factor influencing school and pupil performance, but the sheer, relentless, devastating logic of that reality has become clearer than ever. Attainment follows affluence and pass rates map postcodes. Those with the heaviest burdens face the greatest barriers. The system works for who it works for.

The truth about Scottish schools is that it's not just about classrooms – it's also about class.

Timeline of Scottish Schooling

1496   WORLD LEADERS
            Scotland becomes the first country in the world to
            make schooling compulsory, although this only
            applies to the eldest sons of landowners.

17th century PARISH SCHOOLS
            The Reformationist attempt to provide a school in
            every parish is largely successful in the Lowlands,
            but far less so in the Highlands.

18th century CULTURAL EXPANSION
            The school system is further expanded into the
            Highlands as attempts to suppress and supplant
            Gaelic culture continue.

1872   EDUCATION ACT
            A system of state schooling is introduced as most
            voluntary and religious schools are brought under
            official control. Schooling is made compulsory
            from ages to 5 to 13.

1888   SCHOOL QUALIFICATIONS
            The Scottish Leaving Certificate is introduced and
            the first ever Highers awarded.

1918   EDUCATION ACT
            Catholic schools are brought into the state system
            but with the Church retaining some control over
            curriculum and staffing.

1962   NEW QUALIFICATIONS
            Updated Highers and new O Grades are introduced

to provide pathways for the increasing numbers of pupils staying at school beyond the leaving age.

1986   STANDARD GRADE
New qualifications are introduced with courses available at three levels: credit, general and foundation. The intention is to ensure that all pupils leave school with recognised qualifications.

1999   DEVOLUTION
With the Scottish Parliament reconvened, education is now fully devolved. Scottish Labour wins the first election with a manifesto that promises to build a 'world class' education system.

2002   NATIONAL DEBATE ON EDUCATION
The government launches a consultation to consider the future of Scottish education, a process which will culminate in the development and delivery of a new national curriculum for schools.

2010   CURRICULUM FOR EXCELLENCE
The implementation period of the new curriculum officially begins as the previous 5–14 system is replaced. New S1 pupils will be the first to sit reformed qualifications in 2014.

2020/21   THE PANDEMIC ERA
Schools are closed by the first Covid lockdown and do not reopen for most pupils before summer. The government apologises for an unfair exam replacement system. Further Covid disruption continues into 2021 with a second national schools closure and the cancellation of exam diets.

A (Very) Brief History of Scottish Schools

SCOTLAND'S SCHOOLS USED to be the envy of the world, right? Home of the 'lad o' pairts', that boy of humble means who pulls himself up by his muddy bootstraps, using the power of education to transcend his circumstances and climb the social ladder. It's a good story, but was it ever true? Yes and no. Mostly no. In fact – despite assertions to the contrary – it is probably truer now than it ever was in those largely imagined idyllic years.

Before we start digging into the latest data and deconstructing Curriculum for Excellence, or asking questions about where Scottish education is going, it probably makes sense to be a little bit clearer about how we got to where we are just now.

Pre-20th Century

In 1496 Scotland became the first country to make schooling compulsory, although this applied only to the first-born sons of landowners rather than to the population as a whole. Throughout the 1600s the Reformationist model of parish schools, which received funding from landowners and provided instruction in religion and literacy, was successfully expanded. For some, these schools were also a route to universities, hence the eventual development of the 'lad o' pairts' myth of social progress. Although the system opened up avenues for some it was still a long way from being genuinely meritocratic, with the greatest benefits still out of reach to the poor.

Although the target of a school in every parish had been largely met in the lowlands by the end of the 17th century, the same was not true in the Highlands – but during the 18th century the broader push to suppress and supplant Gaelic culture was continued in part through schools teaching classes in English, many of them run by the Society in Scotland for Propagating Christian Knowledge.

The 1872 Education (Scotland) Act finally brought a wide range of voluntary, philanthropic and religious schools under the shared control of the Scotch Education Department and locally elected boards, thus establishing a genuine system of 'state education'. The Act also made schooling compulsory for children aged 5 to 13, and the leaving age would be raised by another year by the beginning of the next century.

The first Highers were awarded in 1888 as part of the newly introduced Scottish Leaving Certificate.

20th Century

With the passage of the 1918 Education (Scotland) Act, Roman Catholic schools were finally brought into the state system, although the Church retained some control over areas such as curriculum and staffing. Education authorities, which replaced the elected boards, were required to provide secondary schooling for all, but this was initially based on a selective system admitting a minority of children following an examination at 12 years old.

By the middle of the century the school leaving age had reached 15, and post-war social changes meant that an ever-increasing number of pupils were staying on. In response, the qualifications available to school pupils were reformed, with Ordinary Grade – usually known as O Grade – examinations introduced in 1962. The school leaving age was increased to 16 in 1973. By the mid-'80s new Standard Grades – structured in Foundation, General and Credit levels – replaced O Grades. Designed to ensure that everyone left school with some qualifications, their introduction was initially hampered by the industrial dispute over pay and conditions between teachers and the Thatcher government, which ran from 1984 to 1986.

In the final years of the 20th century, academic and vocational qualifications in Scotland were brought together under the umbrella of the newly formed SQA, while reforms known as Higher Still led to the introduction of new courses as part of attempts to develop a 'unified curriculum and assessment system'.

The Post-Devolution Era

When the Scottish Parliament was reconvened in 1999, a Labour and Liberal Democrat coalition formed what was then known as the Scottish Executive. Education in Scotland had always been distinct from provision in other parts of the UK, but it would now become a formally and fully devolved issue – sadly, it would also go on to become a dominant and bitterly politicised issue throughout the parliament's childhood and adolescence.

Little more than a year after the first Scottish election, one of the new parliament's early achievements was the abolition of homophobic legislation, widely known as Section 28, which barred schools from 'promoting homosexuality'. The law was struck down after a 99 to 17 vote, with the Scottish Conservatives opposing the change and both Winnie and Fergus Ewing of the SNP choosing to abstain. This early success, which was important for both practical and symbolic reasons, was achieved despite a vicious 'Keep the Clause' campaign which even included a (failed) private postal referendum funded by one-time SNP donor Brian Souter. But just a few weeks later a scandal broke as failures at the SQA meant thousands of young people received inaccurate or incomplete exam results. It took months to properly identify and tackle the problems, during which time the education secretary was replaced and the existing SQA board swept away.

2002 saw the launch of the 'national debate' as part of a review into Scottish schooling. Over the coming years, this process would eventually lead to the development of a whole new initiative intended to transform the quality of education in the country: the replacement of the old 5–14 system with Curriculum for Excellence (CfE). The new curriculum was dogged by problems throughout both its design and implementation stages but, despite significant concerns, CfE was officially introduced in 2010, the year when the first students due to sit new exams (to be available from 2014) started secondary school.

In March 2020, all schools in Scotland were closed as part of efforts to combat the coronavirus pandemic. Most pupils would not return before the new school year began in August. Exams were cancelled, and an alternative system based on statistical moderation of grades submitted by teachers was put in place. In August, education secretary John Swinney was forced into a humiliating apology before parliament when it became clear that this process had discriminated against pupils from poorer areas. The approach was abandoned, and all reductions to the original, teacher-assigned grades were reversed.

Schools reopened as normal in August, but months of increasing disruption culminated in a second national closure, and the commencement of remote learning, from January 2021. A gradual reopening prioritising the youngest pupils followed. When schools did fully reopen many students in S4–6 found themselves facing an intense and controversial assessment schedule to replace the national exams that had been cancelled months earlier.

2

A Curriculum for Excellence?

IT IS IMPOSSIBLE to analyse the current state of Scottish schooling without understanding the system that underpins it: the supposed Curriculum for Excellence. Too often, however, discussions regarding the curriculum are riddled with assertions and inaccuracies, not least the claim that the entire project was some malign nationalist scheme instigated by the SNP.

So, before we go any further, let's set the record straight.

Origins of CfE

Scottish education has always been distinctive and independent from provision in the UK as a whole, but with the advent of devolution, and return of the Scottish Parliament, it was inevitable that even greater attention would fall on schools. Responsibility for education was, alongside healthcare, one of the most important policy areas controlled by the new Scottish Executive (since given the more appropriate name of the Scottish Government), and while English schools were being directed towards the new Academies programme developed by the UK Labour Party, Scotland – led by a Labour and Liberal Democrat coalition – followed a different path.

In 2002, a 'national debate on education' was launched in order to spark a serious discussion about the future of schooling in the country. It asked about the sort of big-picture issues that are rarely, if ever, considered, rather than directing people to provide narrow responses to a series of overly restrictive questions. More than 20,000 people from a wide range of backgrounds participated in the national debate, offering their opinions on what was working well, what needed to change and, ultimately, what education should be for.

In (very) general terms, the responses revealed continuing support for Scotland's comprehensive and non-selective system of schooling, but also highlighted the need for greater flexibility in the curriculum. Another key outcome was the acceptance that assessment, at all levels, required significant reform. Put simply, it was felt that the existing curricular framework, known as 5–14, meant that too much time was spent testing children, rather than teaching them, and that the focus of these assessments was too narrow. National testing was seen as particularly problematic and restrictive, constraining children's educational experiences in pursuit of ever-improving statistics.

As Scotland moved into the 21st century, and its new parliament began to flex its muscles, the time had come for a new approach to educating its children.

The Design of the Curriculum

It is one thing to decide that things must change – actually making it happen is something else entirely. The existing 5–14 curriculum was seen as too proscriptive and restrictive, and a central goal of reforming it was to free teachers from this sort of bureaucracy and allow them to get on with actually teaching the young people in their care. But some form of framework is still required to outline what young people will learn, when they will learn it, and how that learning will be recognised.

Scotland's new curriculum was supposed to support learning not from the ages of 5–14 but rather from 3–18, meaning that CfE would – at least in theory – offer a coherent but flexible learning experience from the early years right through to the end of secondary school. The idea was to equip young people with 'the knowledge, skills and attributes needed for life in the 21st century' – and that was a goal that attracted a level of broad social and cross-party support that seems unthinkable today. Unfortunately, the more CfE was developed the further it seemed to stray from those early ambitions, a problem which emerged out of a series of fundamental errors throughout the process and for which there is plenty of blame to spread around.

It all begins with the 'four capacities', which sit at the very heart of the curriculum and describe not what we want pupils to learn but rather who we want them to become: successful learners, confident individuals, responsible citizens and effective contributors. A successful learner will, for example, have 'enthusiasm and motivation' and will be able to 'think creatively and independently'; a responsible citizen will have 'respect for others' and the ability to 'develop informed, ethical views of complex issues'; confident individuals will possess 'a sense of physical, mental and emotional wellbeing' and be able to 'assess risk and make informed decisions'; and effective contributors will show 'an enterprising attitude' while they 'solve problems' and 'apply critical thinking in new contexts'.

The fundamental principle of designing a school curriculum around these sorts of attributes is by no means unique to Scotland but these broad – some may say vague – statements with interchangeable descriptors have become a lightning rod for critics of CfE who bemoan a lack of detail and, they claim, rigour.

After the four capacities come the 'seven principles of curricular design': challenge and enjoyment, breadth, progression, depth, coherence, relevance, and personalisation and choice. While developing their plans to ensure that the four capacities are explored and attained, teachers are expected to take these seven principles into account. This takes place across the eight curricular areas of languages (including English literacy and foreign languages), maths, sciences, expressive arts, social studies, technologies, health and wellbeing, and religious and moral education. Primary teachers are of course responsible for all of this but the drive for cross-curricular learning meant that even in secondary schools the areas of literacy, numeracy and health and wellbeing would be regarded as the 'responsibility of all'.

There was also a series of five 'Building the Curriculum' papers to consider (the latter is in five parts and the whole collection runs to hundreds and hundreds of pages) and, later, dozens of Principles and Practice documents described as 'essential reading for practitioners'.

But for all that paperwork there was actually very little detail, demands for which became stronger as the intended implementation date crept closer. As a consequence, the curriculum was broken down into the now infamous 'Experiences & Outcomes': a vast, overlapping array of 'I can...' statements that begin to define the things that students should be able to do and, often only by extension, the things that they should know.

There are more than one thousand 'Es & Os' across five levels covering nine curricular areas at early years (level 0), primary 1–3 (level 1), primary 4–7 (level 2) and s1–3 (levels 3 and 4). Here are a few examples:

Literacy 3-21a
I can use a range of strategies and resources and spell most of the words I need to use, including specialist vocabulary, and ensure that my spelling is accurate.

Numeracy 1-07b
Through exploring how groups of items can be shared equally, I can find a fraction of an amount by applying my knowledge of division.

Health & Wellbeing 2-23a
While working and learning with others, I improve my range of skills, demonstrate tactics and achieve identified goals.

Science 0-06a
I have experienced the wonder of looking at the vastness of the sky, and can recognise the sun, moon and stars and link them to daily patterns of life.

While the Es & Os can generally be made to make sense by professionals they nonetheless feel like they have been designed to be obtuse, almost as if the real goal all along was an exponential multiplication of teachers' workload. It's not even that they're wrong – young children *should* experience the wonder of looking at the vastness of the sky, and we *should* value that sort of experience as much as any other, but in trying to atomise the curriculum down to this sort of level, those responsible seriously undermined the freedoms that were supposed to be at the heart of the reforms.

The Es & Os are a particularly good example of what went wrong with CfE. Worries about a lack of specificity were addressed not through exemplification but rather by a process of itemisation – instead of examples to look at teachers were basically being given boxes to tick. This caused problems not just because the information being provided was *still* too vague but also because it encouraged an audit-driven culture in classrooms.

For years after the launch of the Es & Os teachers raised concerns about the workload implications of an approach built on micro-management rather than trust. In some schools, staff went through the laborious process of 'unpacking' all those curricular organisers, breaking them down to even more minute levels, at the behest of management. Inevitably, the whole thing became an exercise in performative form-filling, with Es & Os shoe-horned into learning experiences – recorded in a planner, written on the board or stickered into a jotter – just to keep the powers that be happy, and whole new IT frameworks (there was even a website called The CfE Machine) being developed to record the information.

The people in charge did eventually accept that the Es & Os were not working – but their solution was the development of an even more extensive list of 'benchmarks' to explain what they meant. So in sciences, for example, outcome 2–15a ('By contributing to investigations into familiar changes in substances to produce other substances, I can describe how their characteristics have changed') was simplified through a transformation into five separate benchmarks:

- Investigates and explains physical changes to the properties of materials which are fully and partially reversible, for example, salt dissolving in water, chocolate melting and water freezing.
- Uses scientific vocabulary such as 'melting', 'freezing', 'evaporating' and 'condensing' to describe changes of state.
- Investigates and records chemical changes to the properties of materials which are irreversible, for example, cooking, rusting and striking a match.
- Observes and identifies some of the signs of a chemical reaction, for example, production of bubbles, colour/texture change and heat given out/taken in.
- Explores and describes the characteristics of solids, liquids and gases, for example, solids retain the same volume and shape, liquids keep the same volume but the shape changes to fit the container and that gases change shape and volume to fill the container.

That the people in charge were unable to see just how ludicrous this whole process was says a great deal about the quality of leadership in Scottish education.

CfE expects teachers to not just deliver a curriculum but to actively construct, review and develop it, all within the context of their own school and with their own pupils in mind. And then at some point we'd also like them to find the time to actually teach the kids, if that's not too much trouble. The sheer volume of workload and expectation was never understood by the people running the show, presumably because they weren't the ones who would actually be in classrooms trying to make it all work, and that critical mistake meant that any idea of a transformation in Scottish schooling was already out of reach before CfE really got going.

Imperfect Implementation

Officially, implementation of CfE took place in 2010, because this was the year in which the first pupils due to sit the new exams in 2014 would enter secondary school. Those changes to senior school qualifications are worth explaining.

Prior to the reforms, the vast majority of students sat eight Standard Grades, which they completed over third and fourth year and which allowed them to be presented at two levels: everyone sat the middle level (General) paper, with some then also attempting the higher level (Credit) and others completing the lower level (Foundation). This dual-entry system worked well for students operating at the boundaries between the levels by ensuring that everyone had something to aim for and a safety net if they didn't quite manage it. Those who achieved Credit level (grades one or two) would generally move on to study up to five Highers, while those with General (grades three or four) or Foundation levels (grades five or six) had the option of completing Intermediate courses, which were designed as both standalone (and well respected) qualifications *and* a stepping-stone to the next levels if appropriate. A relatively small number of pupils also completed other courses like Advanced Highers.

With the introduction of CfE, both the Standard Grade and Intermediate frameworks were swept away, replaced by qualifications known as Nationals: National 5 is, at least officially, broadly equivalent to a Credit Standard Grade or Intermediate 2; National 4 covers the General Standard Grade and Intermediate 1; and National 3 is comparable to a Foundation Standard Grade. Highers and Advanced Highers were retained but reformed.

The changes have been controversial for several reasons. First of all, the transfer to National 4 from General Standard Grade remains contested, with many teachers insistent that a pass at National 4 is by no means equivalent to a grade 3 under the old system. National 4 and below also do not have final exams or even grades, with success instead measured on a pass or fail basis through the completion of internal assessments and a final 'Added Value Unit'. An exam-free approach to qualifications is perfectly workable (colleges, for example, make extensive use of it) but only applying it to the 'lower' qualifications inevitably led to accusations that a two-tier system had been created.

National 4 should, in theory, provide a stepping-stone for those not quite ready for National 5, but progression rates in many subjects are incredibly low. Of course, not all National 4 students will be able to move on to National 5, just as not all National 5 students are able to move on to Higher, but for those who are able there is a feeling that the National 4 is letting them down. At the same time, the lack of grades means that some who complete National 4 may move on to National 5 when they are not, in fact, ready to do so.

The switch to Nationals also affected the significant number of pupils who achieved a General Standard Grade and then used the Intermediate pathway to continue their progression. By removing this alternative qualifications route, CfE-related reforms have arguably narrowed the options available for those young people who do not progress seamlessly into Highers in fifth year.

Using 2010 as the official implementation date for CfE meant that a curriculum that was supposed to transform Scottish schooling, with the goal of recognising the full breadth, depth and value of education from the ages of three to eighteen, was ultimately defined by its relationship to the high-stakes exam system that would continue to dominate those final years of secondary schooling. The tail was already wagging the dog.

Aside from this fundamental, philosophical failure, teachers once again complained – again with justification – about the lack of practical support and exemplification from national bodies. Teachers at all levels were now expected to create their own course assessments in line with the reformed curricular demands. There are plenty of advantages to such a system, not least the ability to integrate assessment into learning in increasingly seamless ways, a process which should also make assessments more reliable by testing what students really know and can do, not the things they've been able to cram into their heads the night before a standalone exam.

It all hinges, however, on teachers having enough confidence to make it work, and that depends on providing them with sufficient support. Key to this is exemplification, where the standards at each level, or for different aspects of a course, are clearly demonstrated. If you show a teacher a good range of examples of what is expected then they can make a brilliant, bespoke course that is both supportive and challenging, but if all you do is hand over page after page of vague and repetitive guidance you achieve the opposite, because the lack of clarity pushes teachers towards safety-first, belt-and-braces tactics built on existing resources and approaches.

Councils made the problems worse by insisting on bureaucratic 'tracking and monitoring' systems that revealed their basic lack of trust in the teaching profession. This was best exemplified through the demand that every pupil at every stage be continuously graded as either 'Developing, Consolidating or Secure' at the relevant curricular level for their age. These sorts of approaches made massive demands on teachers' time, undermined the very principles of the new curriculum, and drove schools even further towards a grim, audit-based, get-all-the-boxes-ticked culture that did nothing to improve the capacity of teachers and certainly damaged the experiences of pupils.

Another common criticism of the implementation of CfE is that those who raised concerns about the structure of the curriculum, or the approaches being adopted, were simply ignored in favour of those who could help to maintain the positive narrative. There was, and remains, a feeling that those in charge of the system are only interested in the opinions of those who will tell them what they want to hear, the sort of people that I once heard described, quite brilliantly, as the 'tooth polishers' of Scottish education.

The obvious problem is that dismissing criticism, whether it is because of defensiveness, a failure to grasp the issues at hand, or the desire to secure the next promotion, is a disastrous way to run an education system. Teachers warned for years about workload implications, the lack of support, and a host of other developing problems but were all too often ignored. As we will see later, a significant number of experienced staff left the profession over the last ten years and, anecdotally at least, problems linked to CfE are often cited as a factor in these decisions.

For all the mistakes that were made, however, there is another massive issue that affected the implementation of CfE, and it is one that is far too often overlooked.

Following a hung parliament in the 2010 UK General election, a Conservative and Liberal Democrat coalition responded to the 2008 financial crisis by imposing austerity on (most of) the population. Driven by right-wing ideology rather than economic necessity, it was an attempt to balance the books on the backs of the poor, further concentrating wealth and power in the hands of a few. In the years that followed the social fabric of the UK was ravaged: as ever, the poorest paid the highest price while those with most just took more and more.

Socialism for the rich and disaster for the rest.

It was against this backdrop that CfE was implemented. That matters. Punitive changes to the welfare state, real terms pay cuts, rising unemployment, the explosion in food bank use and the cynical lie of David Cameron's *Big Society* did untold harm to the lives of huge numbers of pupils and their parents, with the greatest burdens falling, as ever, on the most vulnerable. Child poverty rates, which had fallen throughout the 1990s, have risen since around 2010. A quarter of Scottish children are affected, and two thirds of that group even live in working households. It is increasingly the case that the work available to some members of society – such as those trapped in insecure and exploitative zero-hours employment or denied a real living wage – does not allow them to live free of the scourge of poverty.

CfE had been conceived and designed in a time of plenty but now more and more pupils were coming to school cold or tired or hungry or scared. Cuts meant that teachers (many struggling with their own circumstances) and schools could do less and less for kids exactly when they needed more help than ever. This, combined with all of the existing errors, as well as the enormous challenges inherent to the CfE approach, sailed us straight into a perfect storm from which we have never really been able to escape.

Has Curriculum for Excellence Failed?

It has become fashionable, particularly (but by no means exclusively) amongst political opponents of the SNP, to declare that CfE has failed.

Some point to national and international data – such as literacy rates or the OECD's Programme for International Student Assessment (PISA) scores – as evidence for their positions (more on that later), while others attack the alleged elevation of skills (the things pupils can do) over a more traditionalist focus on knowledge (the things pupils should know). It is not uncommon to hear teachers complain that CfE simply became an exercise in bureaucracy, or parents decry the imposition of a system that they find much more difficult to understand. Some elements of CfE, such as the move away from a single national approach to the number of subjects studied in secondary school, have seen postcode lotteries emerge across the country as councils and even individual schools adopt differing approaches.

What's more, the only serious structural change brought about by CfE was (at least theoretically) delaying the point at which secondary students make subjects choices and begin to progress through qualifications. The goal was to limit the influence of exam pressures on young people's education but in reality, the opposite has been achieved.

The old system used what is commonly referred to as a 2+2+2 structure: the first two years of secondary school featured a general education covering all the different curricular areas; third and fourth year was the period in which pupils worked through eight Standard Grades; and the final two years are when they would focus on Highers, Intermediates or Advanced Highers. In theory, the new structure was to be 3+3: a Broad General Education (BGE) would cover the first three years, and be followed by a 'senior phase' in which qualifications would be completed. However, the removal of two-year Standard Grade courses means that the reality is often rather different, and many argue that our secondary schools effectively operate under a 3+1+1+1 system in which each year of the senior phase is completely dominated by an annual, high-stakes race towards final exams.

There is plenty of truth to all of these criticisms – but does any of it mean that CfE has failed?

There is absolutely no doubt that the current reality of Curriculum for Excellence falls short of the initial, lofty ambitions that accompanied its development. Scottish education certainly doesn't appear to be much more 'excellent' than it was under the old system. But the bureaucratic final form of the curricular structures, coupled with the failures during the implementation stage, and magnified by both the devastating effects of austerity and the reluctance of those in charge to even acknowledge problems as they arose, arguably mean that we have never really seen a Curriculum for Excellence.

Even so, there are countless examples of wonderful, innovative and engaging classroom practice that have been developed using the framework of CfE; speaking from a position of a little bit of experience, however, I certainly always found that the best lessons I delivered to my classes followed the spirit of the curriculum rather than the letter.

The sad, overall reality is that a system that was supposed to free teachers and pupils from red tape ended up binding them in it. What's more, the (cowardly) failure to attempt more than a minimal reform of end of school exams, whilst allegedly transforming everything that came before them, meant that the supposed 3–18 curricular model of CfE actually largely ground to a halt at the age of 15. This meant that there would always be a limit to whatever good could be achieved.

The openness of the curriculum has also had a clear impact. The intention was to allow schools operating in different areas, and within difference contexts, to design their curriculum for the benefit of their own pupils, but too many teachers and too many schools felt that they never received the support needed to make that a reality – many believe that they were simply abandoned, and that the failure to produce a proper framework of resources led to teachers all over the country reinventing the same wheels over and over again. As a result of all this, some schools have undergone something like a transformation over the last decade or so while others, for various reasons, are operating in much the same way as they did in the pre-CfE era.

A further issue caused by the inherent freedom of CfE, and

the failure to properly exemplify different levels of work, is the ongoing concern that standards may no longer be uniform across the country. A teacher in Kirkcudbright might develop one approach to assessing literacy at level 2 while a teacher in Kirkwall develops another, and although there were grand plans to have effective systems of local, regional and national collaboration and moderation underpinning all of this variety they never really came to fruition. This specific failure certainly damaged faith in the reliability of the system overall, a point effectively conceded by the government in 2015, although their attempted solution – to impose national standardised testing on children as young as four – was an enormous and obvious mistake that did nothing to address the fundamental problem.

Perhaps worst of all, the ever-increasing politicisation of Scottish education – for which all parties and a sizeable chunk of the press are responsible – and the sheer mediocrity of those running the system, have made it incredibly difficult, maybe even impossible, for the positives and negatives to be honestly identified over the last decade. We missed chance after chance to learn from successes and resolve problems because those in charge turned out to be utterly incapable of doing the one thing that should always have been the top priority: learning lessons.

But that doesn't mean that the solution is to simply 'scrap' CfE, as some claim. Such a demand isn't coherent on even the most basic level: we can't throw out the entire curriculum overnight and leave a blank space instead, nor would we be able to magically restore the old 5–14 approach that has been gone for more than a decade. There is simply no capacity in the system to instantly replace CfE and, at least so far, no serious alternative to put in its place. There are always people happy to wring their hands and wail that *something must be done*, but solutions are a lot harder to find.

And yet, *something* must be done.

Even before the enormous impact of the coronavirus

pandemic, it was painfully clear that new approaches were needed. Recently, attempts have been made to provide a 'refreshed narrative' for CfE, highlighting successes and setting the original goals of the curriculum 'within the current context'. But nearly two decades on from its origins, and with all the problems that have developed in that time, it doesn't feel like retelling the story of CfE is really going to cut it. We need something more extensive than a fresh coat of paint.

Effective, deep-rooted curricular reform would of course take time but, in the short-to-medium term, one possible solution would be to massively condense the Experiences and Outcomes. Another (better) solution could be to abandon them entirely, and to replace their labyrinthian demands with shorter and clearer expectations of what young people should know and do at each level. Coupled with more specific exemplification, produced at a national level by teams of experts, this sort of change could be achieved relatively quickly – at least when compared to how long the development of an entirely new curriculum would take – and could mitigate some of the biggest issues with the current model of CfE.

Such changes could be the beginning of a process that must naturally end with either the development or eventual replacement of the curriculum. This is not as extreme as it may sound. It has been nearly 20 years since the National Debate on Education was launched in 2002. Back then, *Star Wars Episode II* was one of the biggest films of the year, the Euro had just been introduced as a physical currency, and Henrik Larsson was scoring 35 goals a season for a Celtic team that would soon contest a European final. It was, I think we can agree, quite some time ago. Whether we consider areas such as technology (the internet), science (climate change) or social attitudes (LGBTQ+ rights), it is undeniable that our world has changed massively over that period – and that is before we even begin to factor in the impact of a pandemic that must surely force a reassessment of our priorities?

Curriculum for Excellence was meant to be a radical reform of Scottish schooling but in the end it became just the replacement of one curriculum with another, all within nearly identical structures, but with less support than ever before. It was inevitable that it wasn't going to work. An overnight replacement of CfE is not on the table, but some sort of transformation will ultimately still be needed.

Teachers know how to teach. They're really good at it, and they want to do the best they can for our kids. The great tragedy of CfE has been that, despite all the good intentions, it has all too often stopped teachers from getting on with their job. That's a problem that we desperately need to solve.

3

Closing the Attainment Gap

IF YOU'VE TAKEN the slightest interest in Scottish education or politics over the last few years, and probably even if you haven't, then you will recognise the phrase: 'closing the attainment gap'. It's everywhere, popping up in everything from official reports and parliamentary speeches to newspaper articles and adverts for tutoring companies. But what does it actually mean, why does everyone seem so obsessed with it, and is it really closing?

What is the Attainment Gap?

Put simply, an attainment gap is a difference in outcomes between two groups. Is Group A recording better literacy levels, exam results or even university entries than Group B every year? Yes? Well congratulations – you've found an attainment gap. Most of the time when you see people discussing 'the attainment gap' they are referring to the difference between the richest and poorest pupils, something that some have taken to specifying as the 'poverty-related attainment gap'. So, if 75% of the richest kids achieve a particular benchmark while only 25% of the poorest manage to do the same, we would say that there is an attainment gap of 50 percentage points between the two groups.

However, the principle of an attainment gap means that it is not restricted only to the divides generated by wealth and poverty: differences between boys and girls, different ethnic groups, those with and without additional support needs, and a whole range of other factors can also be understood as attainment gaps. As some of the analysis on subsequent pages will show, Scotland has plenty of these sorts of divides as well, and even when most of our attention is drawn to the glaring gaps between the richest and poorest pupils, it's important that we do not forget that other gaps exist or ignore the various ways in which they intersect with one another.

Why the Focus?

Following the 'No' vote in the 2014 independence referendum, First Minister Alex Salmond had stepped down and was replaced by his deputy, Nicola Sturgeon; soon after, her party won almost every single Scottish seat in the 2015 UK general election, going from six MPs to 56, and claiming an overwhelming victory that reshaped the landscape of the nation's politics.

But all was not well. The government was coming under increasing pressure over its education policies, with ongoing problems with Curriculum for Excellence being brought into sharper relief than ever by the way in which new qualifications had been introduced in secondary schools. To make matters worse, data from the SSLN suggested that standards across earlier levels of schooling were in decline.

In response, the First Minister decided to try to get on the front foot. In August 2015, she went to Wester Hailes Education Centre, a small secondary school in one of the most deprived parts of Edinburgh, and delivered a speech that warped the terms of the education debate for years to come. Sometimes referred to as the 'judge me on my record' speech (although that precise form of words was never uttered), Nicola Sturgeon declared that her government would 'close the attainment gap completely'.

'Let me be clear,' she added. 'I want to be judged on this'.

It was entirely and transparently cynical: political manoeuvring dressed up as a promise of accountability. Nobody disputes the fact that schools are political, but this was an act of brazen politicisation from Scotland's First Minister. It was that simple.

But the problems went far beyond the posturing rhetoric – Nicola Sturgeon also used her speech to announce that these goals would be achieved, at least in part, through the publication of an array of school-level data, including the scores from a new suite of standardised tests that would be imposed on children as young as four years old. Asked whether this would simply ensure the return of a destructive league tables culture, one of the very things that CfE had been developed to avoid, she insisted that she had no intention of publishing such material while accepting that there would be nothing to stop others from doing so. On the day this book went to print, *The Times* newspaper used this data to publish primary school league tables.

This sort of approach is predicated on the assumption that educational outcomes will be improved through competition between schools and, ultimately, their fear of being publicly shamed for results. It was a policy that the Scottish Conservatives (and even Scottish Labour) had demanded, and its adoption was a stark reminder of the SNP's political instincts when it comes to schools.

Ever since that day, Scottish schools have been drawn into an ever more poisonous conflict that plays out on an almost daily basis in the papers, on the television, and across the debating chamber.

Following the Money

Much of the rhetoric around closing the attainment gap is ultimately focused on funding, and in recent years new mechanisms have been put in place to manage the processes by which money is spent on schooling.

The vast majority of funding for schools comes from the local authorities responsible for running them, but the bulk of that council funding comes from the Scottish Government. A recent Audit Scotland report showed that overall council funding in the year 2019/2020 had increased but confirmed that cuts to council budgets in the years previous had been severe. Crucially, they had also been deeper than those faced by the Scottish Government itself.

Additional money for schools is provided through the government's Attainment Scotland Fund (ASF), although this still represents only a small proportion of overall spending. The ASF distributes extra cash to nine 'challenge authorities' (Clackmannanshire, Dundee, East Ayrshire, Glasgow, Inverclyde, North Ayrshire, North Lanarkshire, Renfrewshire and West Dunbartonshire) chosen because of their high levels of social deprivation, as well as a number of specific schools outwith those areas which, according to the government, 'have been identified on the basis of supporting a significant proportion of pupils and families from communities which are facing some of the greatest challenges'.

To make things even more complicated, targeted funding is also provided to schools via the Pupil Equity Fund, which is essentially a Scottish Government branded version of the Pupil Premium introduced in England in 2011. Almost every school receives some PEF money, with the exact amount determined by the number of pupils eligible for free school meals between primary 1 and S3. The total PEF allocation is £120m per year, but this is part of the overall Attainment Scotland Fund.

In theory, all of these funding streams are supposed to help 'close the attainment gap', but the rhetoric doesn't necessarily match the reality: there are ongoing concerns about the effectiveness of the models being used, which at times make it much harder to be sure of what is really going on across the country.

Although there are plenty of examples of schools making effective use of PEF allocations (*see the work of Lochend*

Community High School and Bellahouston Academy highlighted later) it remains incredibly difficult to properly assess how the money is being spent, although some anecdotal examples – such as that of the consultant who was paid around £1000 a day for two weeks work from a local PEF allocation – have certainly raised concerns.

Even where comparatively robust information is available it can often generate more questions than answers. Take, for example, the way in which PEF money is being spent to increase teacher numbers. According to a Scottish Government FOI response, this model now funds more than one thousand teaching posts across the country, but around half of them are on temporary contracts and nearly two thirds are part-time. Furthermore, around a fifth of these jobs are actually promoted posts, although this is perhaps not surprising – a relatively common complaint from teachers is that some PEF money has been spent creating new jobs that come with fancy titles but offer little real value to the school or pupils, with the primary benefit being enjoyed by the (often fairly young) members of staff having their bank balances and CVs enhanced. I have spoken to teachers who told me that they held PEF-funded posts but had never seen a job description.

The government insists that the Pupil Equity Fund has been a success, but there remains little recognition of the concerns and drawbacks. What sort of additional workload does it create for already over-stretched staff? Should schools need to make funding trade-offs, deciding whether to run breakfast clubs or employ another teacher? Does the PEF model encourage a creeping form of privatisation where outside organisations are encouraged to approach schools and effectively bid for some of the pot? More than £100m of 'anti-poverty funds' will always make for good headlines but is it really the best model, particularly after years of cuts to council budgets and in a system with finite resources?

In a properly resourced system PEF would be a fantastic bonus; when schools are massively over-stretched, it can feel like little more than an attempt to paper over some of the many cracks.

Is the Gap Closing?

It is worth noting that the government's language around 'closing the gap' has shifted since 2015. We were initially told that the SNP would 'completely' close the gap between rich and poor pupils; by the time their 2016 manifesto was published, this had morphed into a pledge to 'make significant progress in closing the gap within the next parliament and to substantially eliminate it within a decade'. Then, in 2017, these ambitions were themselves substantially reduced, with the government setting targets to narrow a series of specific gaps by just a few percentage points over the following few years. But given the early rhetoric and that original manifesto wording, it is fair to ask whether the gaps have indeed been completely closed, or even 'substantially reduced', over the last five years. Unsurprisingly, the answer is no.

In 2017, official data showed that the primary school attainment gap in literacy stood at just over 22 percentage points, with the government aiming to reduce this to 16 percentage points by 2020. The 2019 data recorded the gap as being 20.6 percentage points, just 1.4 percentage points lower than where it started and nowhere near on track to meet the government's own target. The figures for primary school numeracy show an even smaller decline of less than one percentage point over the same period. Things are just as bad at secondary school level, where the numeracy gap has fallen by just 1.5 percentage points and the literacy gap is effectively unchanged.

Even if we concentrate on the somewhat questionable – but still official – measure of pupils leaving school with one or more

School Leaver Data: Attainment Gaps for One or More Qualifications (SIMD) 2016–2020

Source: Scottish Government, Summary Stats for Attainment and Initial Leaver Destinations; and Scottish Government, 2018 National Improvement Framework and Improvement Plan

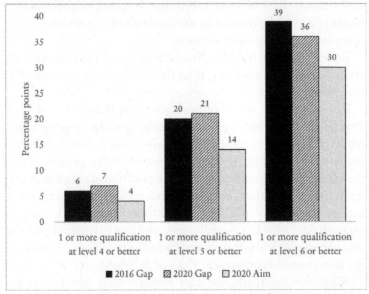

qualifications at particular levels, the picture does not improve. At levels 4 and 5 the attainment gap between least and most affluent has very slightly increased; at level 6 it has dropped a little but remains both enormous and well in excess of the government's aim.

Of course, you may ask whether any of this is really a surprise. Scotland is no less unequal than it was when everyone started talking about attainment gaps, so why would the gaps themselves have shifted much in that time?

Furthermore, is there really anything to be gained from obsessing over shifts of a few percentage points – or fractions of percentage points – here and there when we already know that this problem is driven by the lived experience of poverty and deprivation rather than variations in a spreadsheet? Social class, not statistical sleight-of-hand, is the issue here, right?

These are fair questions but, having insisted that she wanted to be judged on her record, and then presented this information as the means by which the public could do so, neither the first minister nor her government are in much of a position to start complaining about such scrutiny.

If we are indeed to judge Nicola Sturgeon on her record and, crucially, on *her own terms* then the unavoidable conclusion is that she has failed.

But maybe the more serious question is whether she, or anyone else in positions of power, really thought those promises could be kept. Were they, perhaps, always just rhetoric? Do we really believe that the government simply failed to understand the reality of the problem they were confronting, and that this ignorance lead to them making promises that they would never, ever be able to fulfil? Or do we think that they always knew that their pledges couldn't be delivered, and just calculated that the short-term political advantages of positive headlines outweighed the longer-term reputational risks of falling short?

Whatever the truth, the fact remains that when it comes to the attainment gap, little has changed, or looks likely to change. Hundreds of millions of pounds have been transferred into PEF and other targeted funding; millions more have been handed over to a private company in exchange for a pointless standardised testing system; more attention has been paid to the divides between rich and poor than ever before – but in the end, all the soap-box rhetoric of 2015 and beyond has simply led to even more wasted years.

The truth about 'closing the attainment gap' is simple: it is not, and never has been, much more than a slogan.

4

Making Sense of the Statistics

ONE OF THE biggest problems when discussing the performance and quality of schools in Scotland is that so much of the debate becomes wrapped up in a seemingly endless array of statistics, with all sides apparently able to prove their competing points while holding up the exact same data. Like Schrödinger's Cat, schools seem to simultaneously exist in two contradictory forms: standards are both plummeting and improving; the system is both in terminal decline and in the process of restoring itself to past glories; young people are being failed while also getting the best possible start in life.

It's time to figure out the truth.

But first, we should clarify a key feature of Scottish deprivation data. Whenever you see references to the most and least deprived (or simply the poorest and richest) areas, the numbers are generally being broken down using the Scottish Index of Multiple Deprivation (SIMD). This system uses seven distinct factors – income, employment, health, education, skills and training, geographic access to services, crime, and housing – to rank every part of the country on a scale from one (most deprived) to ten (least deprived).

However, despite SIMD underpinning vast swathes of public policy and statistics, it is by no means perfect. In rural Scotland, SIMD areas can be so large that they hide, rather than highlight, poverty, and across the country it's thought that only around half of low-income families live in the postcodes categorised as most deprived.

In its 2016 Final Report, the Commission on Widening Access noted that 'the main concern expressed on the use of SIMD is that it is an area-based measure and therefore is less likely to capture individual circumstances'. For example, a university that seeks to address inequality by offering additional places to those in those most deprived areas, as measured by SIMD, may end up actually excluding more deprived young people living a few streets away.

Recent work by Professor John Jerrim of University College London has argued that free school meals eligibility – especially the amount of time for which a child has been eligible – is a more reliable measure of young people's backgrounds and its likely impact on their education. This information is potentially available in Scotland but is not routinely utilised.

PISA

Let's start with the numbers that newspapers and opposition politicians love, but which hardly anyone ever bothers to explain: the Programme for International Student Assessment, better known as 'PISA'. Overseen by the Organisation for Economic Co-operation and Development (OECD), PISA 'measures 15-year-olds' ability to use their reading, mathematics and science knowledge and skills to meet real-life challenges'.

The tests have been administered every three years since 2000, alternating between the three focus areas in each cycle, and have come to be seen by some as the definitive measure of educational success: relatively small variations in performance can provoke panic and reactive policy change – sometimes referred to as 'PISA shock' – as pundits, politicians and perhaps even the public demand an immediate response.

But there are well-documented problems with PISA. Writing

for the Washington Post in 2015, renowned international experts Pasi Sahlberg and Andy Hargreaves outlined three specific and serious concerns about the processes and organisations that have come to wield so much power over school systems around the world. In an article entitled 'The Leaning Tower of Pisa', they argue that the current approach of ranking countries has 'negative consequences for school systems' because it encourages countries to depend upon standardised testing and to value only that which can be 'easily measured'. They also believe that the OECD is 'biased in favour of economic interests in public education', with particular attention drawn to its links to international edu-businesses which profit from selling 'PISA-like instruments for practice in school' – and it is worth noting at this point that the Scottish Government's standardised testing programme for schools is purchased from an organisation which had previously administered the PISA tests. Finally, they remind us that the way in which the tests are designed include 'major technical flaws' which undermine the final results.

Nonetheless, they argue that PISA should be reformed rather than abolished, reasoning that, for all its flaws, PISA has also achieved some good for international education. Without it, they insist, countries now regarded as world leaders in schooling, such as Finland and Canada, would never have been recognised, and 'the worldwide pressures for more market competition between schools, less university-based training for teachers, and more standardisation of the curriculum, would have had a far easier ride'. PISA may well have serious underlying issues, but it has also shown us the value of high-quality teacher education and a focus on collaboration, not competition, as the route to improvement.

Others are even more critical of PISA. Yong Zhao, a professor at both the University of Kansas and the Melbourne Graduate School of Education, describes it as a 'masterful magician' that has 'successfully created an illusion of education quality and marketed it to the world.' In a paper entitled *Two decades of havoc: A synthesis of criticism against PISA,* he argues that the model is a 'flawed business that has great power to misguide education'. In 2014, a group of leading experts from around the world signed an open letter to the director of the OECD raising serious concerns about a list of 'negative consequences of the PISA rankings'. The letter highlighted issues such as the programme's contribution to an 'escalation' in standardised testing, the fact that it encourages short-term thinking, the lack of democratic oversight of the OECD, and the links to private companies seeking to profit from national education systems. The authors ultimately argue that 'the new PISA regime, with its continuous cycle of global testing, harms our children and impoverishes our classrooms,' and called – unsuccessfully – for the next testing cycle to be delayed.

PISA may have its place, but it also carries with it a significant risk of serious misuse, particularly when schooling is as politicised as it has become here in Scotland. It has become too easy for political opponents to simply sling stats at one another, and at the public, in the hope that some of the good or bad numbers (depending on which side you're on) happen to stick. If PISA is worth doing then it's worth doing right, which means making accurate and effective use of the potentially valuable data it generates while avoiding the many pitfalls that come with the league tables model.

When the 2018 PISA results were released in December of the following year, the headlines lamented scores that were the 'worst ever' and a 'record low', although the BBC took a more balanced approach and described a 'Mixed report for Scottish education in world rankings'. Unsurprisingly, the Scottish Government's own news release was markedly more optimistic, with 'main messages' such as the country's above-average performance and overall improvement in reading – the main focus of the 2018 assessment series – and continued achievement of scores 'similar to the OECD average' for maths and science.

The truth lies somewhere in the middle, although finding it requires at least a minimal grasp of the nuances of the data; but before we even get to the numbers themselves, we need to be clear about what they do and do not show.

The PISA tests are carried out on a sample of pupils from more than one hundred schools across the country – they are not completed by every pupil in Scotland, which means that national scores need to be calculated from the available data. There is always, therefore, a little bit of doubt about those final figures. This is quite normal, and the data generated by PISA is considered reliable enough that we can be 95% sure the assigned score is correct for the country as a whole, but that still leaves a bit of wiggle room on either side within which the true score may lie. This means that changes from year to year, or differences between one country and another, need to be outside of that margin for error in order to be considered 'statistically significant'. Professor Mark Priestley and Dr Marina Shapira of the University of Stirling have explained this issue particularly well. Questions have also been raised about the reliability of PISA data in Scotland (and, in fairness, the UK as a whole) with a change to the assessment date and low response rates recently flagged by Professor John Jerrim as potentially influencing the results.

So, with those small but crucial caveats in mind, what do the PISA results *really* tell us?

In 2018, Scotland's reading score stood at 504 points, a small but just about significant increase on the 2016 result. It was also broadly similar to levels in 2012, 2009 and 2006, but below the scores in 2003 (516 points) and 2000 (526 points). Using PISA as a measure, we can see that there has been a clear decline in reading standards in Scotland during the devolution era, but that it largely occurred between the years 2000 and 2006, prior to the introduction of Curriculum for Excellence and the SNP's first election victory in 2007. The small increase in 2018 could be a blip, a return to the norm, or a sign of measurable improvement, depending on your preferences or prejudices.

Scotland's mathematics score in 2018 was 489 points. Although it is technically true to say that this is the lowest figure recorded since the tests began more than two decades ago, this is an overly simplistic interpretation. The score has declined from a high of 524 points in 2003 but, as with the drop in reading performance, the real fall took place in the years leading up to 2006. So, while opponents of the SNP would point to the falling absolute scores as evidence of government failure, its supporters might reasonably retort that, as with reading levels, a severe decline in performance has in fact been at least partly arrested since their party took power in 2007.

When it comes to science, however, the pattern changes. The 2018 and 2015 scores were broadly similar, but both represented a notable drop from 2012, 2009 and 2006. In this curricular area, performance appears to have been stable until the period in which Curriculum for Excellence implementation was being completed, at least opening the possibility that something about CfE, whether that be the design or the delivery or a mixture of both, has contributed to falling performance in science amongst 15-year-olds.

So where does all this leave Scotland in comparison to other countries? The 2018 results mean that only Canada, Estonia, Finland, Ireland and Korea registered significantly better reading scores than Scotland, with countries such as New Zealand, Norway, England, Japan and Germany achieving similar results. In maths, a much larger group of 18 countries score statistically higher than Scotland. The same five countries that come top in reading appear once again, joined by nations such as Japan, the Netherlands and Switzerland. Scotland's performance is in fact bang on the OECD average, comparable to countries such

PISA: Scotland's Scores 2000–2018

Source: Scottish Government, Programme for International Student Assessment (PISA) 2018

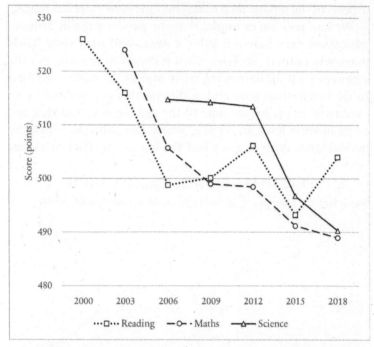

Scotland's performance has declined in all three measures, but the biggest drops in reading and maths scores took place before the introduction of CfE.

as Iceland, France, Wales and Portugal, and ahead of others like the United States and Israel. For science, Scotland's performance was one point above the average of 489, lower than England and 12 others including Germany, Slovenia and the United States, but equal to otherwise 'top performing' Ireland and others such as Austria, Northern Ireland, Denmark and Spain, and higher than that of Iceland, Luxembourg and Italy

You'd be forgiven for not knowing *any* of these important nuances if you were depending upon the way in which PISA is reported in the press. Even at the surface level PISA data is far more complicated than the headlines would have you believe. What's more, if you dig into some of the commonly ignored aspects of the reports then things become even more interesting.

We can see, for example, that the gender gaps in Scottish education vary between subject areas and over time. Girls massively outperform boys when it comes to reading, but the gap appears to be narrowing fairly rapidly. In maths boys tend to do better than girls and, although this gap seemed to be closing in 2015, by the time of the next tests it had returned to its historic level. In science, where boys also do better, the performance drop in 2015 had the knock-on effect of all but

PISA: Scotland's Gender Gaps 2006–2018

Source: Scottish Government, Programme for International Student Assessment (PISA) 2018

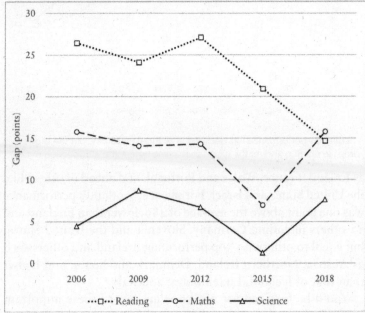

In reading, the gender gap favoured girls whilst in maths and science it favoured boys.

eliminating the attainment gap between boys and girls, but as with the maths figures this gap jumped again three years later.

PISA reports also allow us to compare the level of performance variation within each country, helping us to understand the overall averages in a clearer context. The OECD use a system called the Index of Economic, Social and Cultural Status (ESCS) in order to account for the social background of those responding to their tests. This means that countries can be assigned a value to reflect the extent to which a student's circumstances influence their results.

For reading in 2018, Scotland scored 8% on this measure, roughly the same as a range of countries that includes England, Estonia, Finland, Korea and Latvia, and well ahead of others like Germany (17%), Belgium (17%) France (18%) and Hungary (19%). The data shows that the amount of grade variation in maths attributable to social background in Scotland is also 8%, which in this subject area makes the country a world leader. Even in science, where the impact of students' backgrounds rises slightly, Scotland's score remains close to the 6% that makes Canada and Wales stand out. However, this apparent success can sometimes be understood as a consequence of Scotland's weaker results among the most affluent pupils. For example, the 2018 gap between rich and poor for reading scores was 72 points in Scotland and 79 points in Finland, but the gap is only smaller here because our better-off students didn't do quite as well as theirs.

Are there any simple lessons to learn from PISA? Well, Canada, Estonia, Finland, Korea, Ireland and, arguably, Poland appear to be the 'top' countries, but that doesn't mean we should simply try to replicate their approaches in our own schools. As is always the case with education, policy choices and successes cannot be separated from the context of the society in which they are found. In fact, perhaps the most important thing to remember when it comes to PISA is that simplistic media narratives are rarely accurate but regularly harmful. When you see a politician squeezing the scores into a soundbite, or a columnist breezing over the detail in a couple of sentences, then you can pretty much guarantee that they're not giving you the full story.

The Three Rs

While PISA is designed to provide international comparisons in education data, it is absolutely vital to have sound internal systems for measuring the health of a nation's schools. At the most basic level this means being able to analyse 'the three Rs' ('literacy and numeracy' in new money) that are seen as the basis of all other learning. In Scotland, the need to get this process right has been brutally highlighted by a recent change which showed the government getting things very, very wrong.

Up until 2017, the main source of information for pupil performance at primary and lower secondary (S1–3) levels was the Scottish Survey of Literacy and Numeracy (SSLN). Alternating between the two areas from one year to the next, the SSLN took a sample-based approach to measuring young peoples' abilities by the end of primary four, primary seven and S2. It was also designed to assess performance in line with the expectations of Curriculum for Excellence.

It is important to understand exactly how the SSLN worked to appreciate what made it so valuable. Each year, around ten thousand pupils from across the more than 2,500 schools in Scotland were selected to take part in the short, unseen test papers that made up that year's assessment. There was no way to anticipate which students would be selected but, more importantly, there was no pressure to do so, because the results were not tied to, and thus could not be seen as a judgement on, individual schools or teachers. This was a key strength of the SSLN because it meant that, unlike with so many other metrics, there was no reason to even attempt to game the system and artificially inflate results. There was also no risk of the data being corrupted through misuse or warping what was happening in classrooms because it had a single, simple purpose: to measure performance at a strictly national level. It wasn't designed for school rankings or pupil feedback which means that it did not need to be compromised. The SSLN had one job to do, and it did it well. In fact, in such politicised times it probably sowed the seeds of its own destruction by doing that job too well.

The final SSLN report, published in 2017 from data collected in 2016, focused on literacy levels across Scotland. It revealed that the number of pupils 'working well or very well' at their expected curricular level had either remained broadly stable or, in some specific categories, continued a decline that had been evident since the 2012 survey. Reading levels for primary 4 and primary 7 pupils had not improved over the previous two years, with the former have fallen by six percentage points since the 2012 survey was completed. Although the 2016 figure for s2 pupils was higher than 2014, it was still lower than 2012.

When measuring writing ability, the survey found that primary 4 results had dropped by two percentage points since 2012, with primary 7 results falling by seven percentage points in the same period. However, it was in s2 where the most serious problem seemed to have been discovered: in 2012, 64 percent of pupils had been deemed to be working well or very well at the appropriate level, but by 2016 this figure had plummeted to just 49%.

Looking past the headline figures didn't help either. At every stage, the gap between boys and girls for both reading and writing levels had either remained the same between 2012 and 2016 or – as in most cases – actually increased, with girls doing better than boys. The same pattern emerged when the data was broken down by deprivation levels, although the gaps were much wider, with divides of around 20 points between the richest and poorest primary 7 and s2 pupils when it came to writing.

SSLN: Pupils Working Well or Very Well at Expected Writing Levels 2012–2016

Source: Scottish Government, Scottish Survey of Literacy and Numeracy

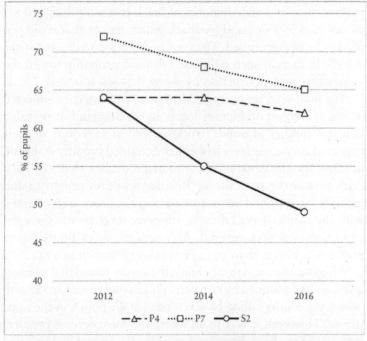

The performance of S2 pupils fell by 15 percentage points in just four years

The 2015 SSLN numeracy results had also caused concern: at primary 4, the number of pupils working well or very well at their expected level fell by 11 percentage points in just four years; the trend for primary 7 results was only slightly better, having fallen by six points in the same period; and while S2 data showed far more stable performance, a massive 60% of pupils at that stage were not making the expected progress for their age group. Once again, gender gaps had barely changed, although boys outperformed girls at every level rather than the other way around.

What's more, the poverty gaps revealed by the data were simply horrifying: 21 percentage points at primary 4 (up from 12 points in 2011); 22 percentage points at primary 7 (up from 16 points in 2011) and 28 percentage points in S2 (identical to the 2011 figure).

Importantly, however, the SSLN surveys also managed to go beyond simple test scores, gathering a range of other valuable

SSLN: Numeracy Rates and Attainment Gaps 2011–2015

Source: Scottish Government, Scottish Survey of Literacy and Numeracy

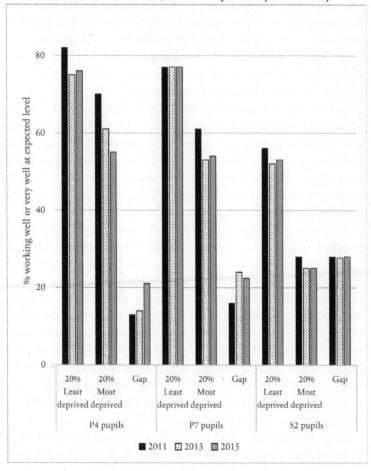

information about pupils' experiences at school, their confidence in their own learning, and their home environments. It also collected data from teachers who talked about their working environments. In 2016, a quarter of primary 4 pupils said that they 'hardly ever or never' had someone read with them at home, and a similar proportion of non-English secondary school teachers were not confident teaching various aspects of reading and writing to their pupils. Nearly 70% of primary school teachers, and more than three quarters of secondary teachers, reported that they had been unable to visit other schools to observe good practice over the previous 12 months. All of this was relevant but, as is so often the case with valuable data, it was generally ignored in favour of a focus on simple, headline-friendly figures.

Either way, the picture painted by the SSLN was, by 2016, becoming brutally clear: when it came to literacy and numeracy levels, the foundations of so much of young people's educations, Scotland was either treading water or going backwards. For a government that had recently demanded to be judged on its record, especially its ability to close the gaps between the richest and poorest pupils, this was a problem.

Of course, the SSLN wasn't perfect. One specific (and valid) criticism was that the system measured pupil performance in S2 but did so relative to curricular benchmarks designed to run until the end of S3. This adds a bit of uncertainty when comparing figures to those of primary 4 and primary 7, where the assessment windows aligned properly with the curriculum, although there are no such doubts over year-on-year comparisons for the S2 data itself. Other people asked if the sample sizes were large enough, argued that the failure to break down results by local authority left a critical piece of the overall puzzle unfilled, or asked whether, like PISA, the SSLN should be expanded to include subject areas like science.

All of these issues could have been addressed as part of steps to strengthen this vital source of data on Scottish schooling;

instead, the SNP decided to scrap the SSLN entirely, and there remains a strong suspicion that this decision was ultimately made because the government didn't like the data being produced. Ending the SSLN effectively allowed those in charge to reset the score, with the rest of us supposed to believe that changing the way we measured progress – or the lack of it – across the country, and preventing proper comparisons over time, would somehow make things better for anyone other than SNP politicians.

Instead of SSLN data, the government now collects and publishes literacy and numeracy stats within the framework of the Achievement of Curriculum for Excellence Levels (ACEL). The information is gathered for pupils in primary 1, primary 4, primary 7 and third year of secondary school, reflecting the transition points between early level, first level, second level and third level CfE expectations. ACEL data provides information on overall literacy and numeracy rates (although the former was not included in the original 2015 data) as well as performance breakdowns in three specific areas of literacy: reading, writing and 'listening & talking'.

The most recent publication provides data for the school year ending in 2019, with the collection and publication of 2020 data cancelled because of the coronavirus pandemic. The primary school results were as follows:

	Pupils meeting expected levels in literacy	Pupils meeting expected levels in numeracy
Primary 1	76%	85%
Primary 4	70%	77%
Primary 7	71%	76%
Primary 1/4/7 (combined)	72%	79%

Most pupils, therefore, are doing well, although it is also certainly the case that very significant minorities of pupils are *not* meeting expected levels – but it doesn't necessarily follow that they are 'failing' or, to address a particularly cynical misrepresentation from recent years, functionally illiterate or innumerate. The whole point of CfE was to allow learners to progress through the curricular levels at their own pace, and as such there is a bit of overlap built in between the levels at the points at which pupils progress from one to another. So while level 2 outcomes are intended for the primary 4–7 years, the expectation was always that the majority of pupils, not all of them, would be able to move on to level 3 as they started high school.

The literacy and numeracy data for secondary schools is slightly more complicated, focusing only on a single stage – S3 – but covering curricular levels 3 and 4. This is because while most pupils are expected to have 'achieved' level 3 by the end of third year, some may also have progressed towards level 4 learning during this period. Although this can be confusing it is also potentially useful, because increased numbers of pupils working at level 4, either nationally or amongst particular groups, could indicate increased readiness for National 5 and Higher courses in the following years.

The 2018/2019 data shows that 88% of S3 pupils achieved level 3 in literacy and 90% did so in numeracy; however, these figures tumble to 48% and 59% at level 4. As ever, different people will interpret those figures in different ways: for some, nine out of ten S3 pupils meeting the expected standards in numeracy will be cause for celebration; for others, less than half making it to level 4 literacy will be a scandal. Others may ask why performance in both literacy and numeracy seems to start off strong, dip throughout primary school, and then rise again in secondary.

These overall figures are good for generating controversy, but they actually don't tell us as much as some might think. In order to really understand what is going on, and whether progress is being made, we need to go beyond the headline data and dive into the breakdowns between different social groups. By analysing ACEL data broken down by deprivation levels, and identifying the gaps that exist, we can gain a far greater understanding of the reality for Scotland's pupils.

That reality is simple: at every single level, for every single area, and in every single year, ACEL data has shown large gaps between pupils from the richest and poorest areas. To make matters worse, and despite the claims of government politicians and officials, there has been little if any significant progress in closing these gaps over recent years – in fact, the gaps have actually widened when analysing pupils' achievement of level four literacy and numeracy standards.

So, by the government's own preferred measure, using a system that it devised, it seems that little if any progress has really been made in terms of 'closing the attainment gap'. Unsurprisingly, however, there are more pressing problems with ACEL data than its tendency to generate bad headlines for the government.

Some remain unconvinced that the information is reliable. Unlike the SSLN, where data was generated by carefully constructed and externally marked assessments, ACEL data is provided by classroom teachers exercising their professional judgement about their own pupils. Teachers are perfectly capable of determining whether or not a student has, for example, met the requirements for level 2 literacy, but only if the standards are made suitably clear. More than a decade on from the implementation of CfE, it is still not evident that this is the case.

Another major problem with the ACEL data is that it attempts to do several jobs at once and, inevitably, ends up doing none of them well. The government seems to believe that this data can be both formative (used to support young people to improve)

ACEL: Literacy and Numeracy Attainment Gaps (SIMD) 2017–2019
Source: Scottish Government, Achievement of Curriculum for Excellence Levels

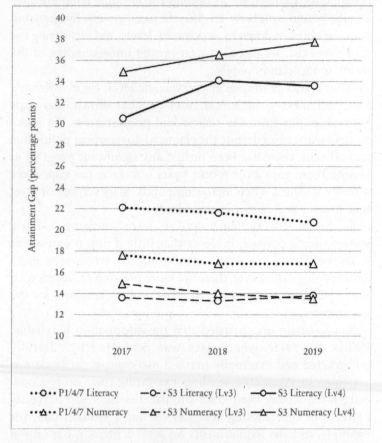

and summative (used to assess overall performance) but it just isn't true, either in principle or in practice.

ACEL judgements, theoretically informed by clumsy and counter-productive standardised tests, are an incredibly blunt tool compared to the precision of proper teacher feedback and therefore serve little if any purpose for pupils. The actual data, published on a school-by-school basis, was supposed to allow for comparisons between schools, but different approaches to gathering information and the negative consequences of such a high-stakes system make this all but impossible to do with any real confidence. Finally, the aggregated data is supposed to show us what is happening at a national level, but the shift away from the sample-based approach of the SSLN introduces unavoidable pressure to game the system (and help the government make itself look better) and undermines the reliability of the information being provided.

Even the switch from 'working well or very well' within a curricular level to 'achieving' it is not the sign of progress that some might assume. People want to think of this sort of information in terms of passing and failing but that isn't a particularly helpful approach, particularly when you remember that we are dealing with broad curricular areas covered by a range of experiences rather than something like a Higher course that has a defined end and a final examination. CfE simply wasn't designed for this sort of black and white interpretation, and attempts to impose this style of simplistic analysis have just caused more problems.

So even though we now gather data for every school, generated by every pupil, we don't actually know any more, and can probably be sure of even less, about the literacy and numeracy levels of children across the country. We also saw both the news cycles and the capacity for public and parliamentary accountability choked up by the change from SSLN to ACEL, a process which provided some protection for struggling politicians while doing absolutely nothing for struggling pupils.

In the end, a government that was supposed to be judged on its record left us less informed than we had been before. Perhaps that was the point all along.

Senior Phase Attainment

We use literacy and numeracy data to measure standards for primary school and the first half of secondary, but in the senior phase of high school attention inevitably turns to the all-important exam results. The simplest way in which to analyse exam success levels is to look at the overall pass rates for key qualifications – in Scotland, that means Highers and, to a lesser degree, National 5s.

Between 2007 and 2020, the pass rate for all Highers increased from 73.3% to 74.9%. The qualifications experienced some changes from 2015 with the introduction of Curriculum for Excellence, so although the names were retained some of the content and assessment approaches were altered. In 2015 both the old and new versions of Highers ran in parallel, with schools and colleges able to choose which they wanted to put their students through. In that first and only year of direct comparisons, the 79.7% pass rate for the new Higher exceeded the 77.1% for the old one – but from then on, the Higher pass rate dropped each year. The exception was 2020, when the cancellation of exams led to an increased pass rate across the board (more on that later), and 2021, when they were pushed back down but remained higher than historic levels. The trend in Higher pass rates since 2007, combining both the old and new qualifications where they overlapped, is shown in the graph on page 65.

Comparing the results for National 5 and its precursors is much more difficult because these new courses replaced a number of pre-existing options across both the old Standard Grade and Intermediate frameworks. To further complicate things, Nationals and Intermediates, like the two versions of Higher, were briefly run in parallel to ease the transition, but the two are not directly comparable because the Intermediate 2 was often provided as a second chance for pupils looking to move from Standard Grade to Higher after failing to attain a Credit grade of 1 or 2. We can, however, take a look at the data since the Nationals were introduced, in order to identify any particular trends.

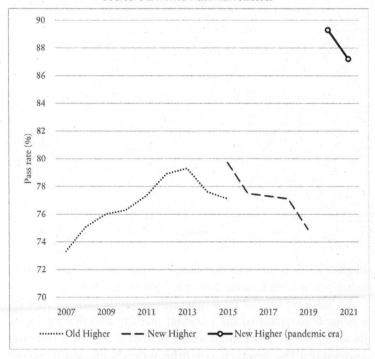

Exam Results: Highers Pass Rate 2007–2021
Source: SQA Annual Attainment Statistics

What we find is that the pass rates for National 5 fell quite significantly (relatively speaking) in the year following its introduction, before first exceeding and then returning to the 2014 levels. This is a good example of why we should never panic over a single dip in our data – the 2015 results now look like a blip but, at the time, could have easily been spun as evidence that the National 5 was a failed qualification. As at

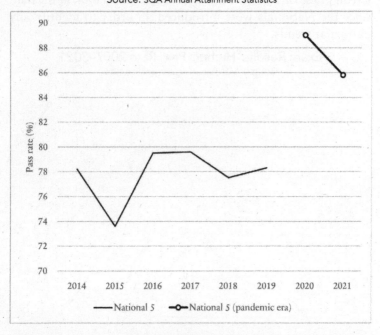

Exam Results: National 5 Pass Rate 2014–2021
Source: SQA Annual Attainment Statistics

Higher level, pass rates significantly improved in 2020 before being pushed back down towards historic levels in 2021.

So, data on overall pass rates can certainly provide us with a general snapshot of the national picture, and that can have its uses, but we need to go much further if we want to really understand the progress, or otherwise, being made across the country, particularly with regards to the attainment gaps between the richest and the poorest pupils.

The Scottish Government's preferred measure for quantifying that gap is counting the number of pupils who leave school each year with one or more qualifications at a particular curricular level. Attention is typically drawn to level 6 because this is where the Highers sit, although it is important to point out that this level also includes several alternative qualifications which may or may not be comparable to Highers, depending on your focus. In 2020, a total of 170,691 level 6 courses were passed by school pupils in Scotland, 95% of which were Highers – but the remaining 5% (a total of just under 9,000 qualifications) were a mixture of different courses offered as part of the Scottish Credit and Qualifications Framework (SCQF).

Crucially, while they all count as level 6 qualifications, they are not valued in the same way. A pupil completing a Higher receives 24 points per qualification; Award courses, available in the areas of Religion, Belief & Value, Leadership, Personal Development, Scots Language, Scottish Studies, and Statistics, are worth between 3 and 34 points; National Certificate courses in Art & Design, Computing with Digital Media, Creative Industries, Dance, Hairdressing, Music, and Social Sciences all earn 72 points; and National Progression Awards – which cover a wide range of specialisms including Acting & Performing, Computer Game Development, Customer Service, Journalism, Laboratory Science, and Sports Development – are worth at least 12 and as many as 120 points. A range of different qualifications are also available at levels 4 and 5.

Qualifications Awarded to School Pupils 2020			
Source: SQA Annual Attainment Statistics			
	Level 4	Level 5	Level 6
National Courses (Nat 4 / Nat 5 / Higher)	93,437	264,344	161,786
Skills for Work	1,102	6,569	0
Awards	9,685	7,972	5,870
National Certificates	0	2	37
National Progression Awards	1,540	3,412	2,998

At a national level there is little harm done by conflating National Courses with all qualifications, at least for levels 5 and 6, because the former makes up the overwhelming majority of certifications for school leavers; however, there is no way of knowing whether these alternative qualifications are spread evenly across the country or if, as seems infinitely more likely, they are found in larger numbers in a comparatively small number of schools. This is just one of the many reasons why the school league tables you see each year in newspapers should never, ever be taken seriously.

Data on the achievement of qualifications is also used each year in relation to school leavers, with the government particularly interested in the number who have secured at least one level 6 qualification during their time at secondary school. In 2020, nearly two thirds of all school leavers had managed this, which represented a significant improvement on 2010 when only half had done so. The number leaving with at least one or more qualification at level 5 or better has also risen in that time while the gaps between the richest and poorest pupils achieving these benchmarks have declined: for level 6, it has fallen from 45.6 percentage points in 2010 to 36.1 percentage points in 2020; at level 5, the gap was cut from 33.3 percentage points a decade ago to 20.8 now.

By this sort of analysis, Scottish education has managed to make some remarkable progress over the last decade, and it's no surprise when government ministers and spin doctors attempt to focus attention on this single – conveniently co-operative – metric when trying to convince us that things are going well. But there's a glaring problem with this data: it is simply far too crude to actually tell us anything useful. Yes, we know how many young people overall now leave school with at least one level 6 qualification, but which qualifications, in what subject areas, and – in the case of Highers at least – with what grades? The official data doesn't help us to answer these important questions because the system counts pupils who leave school with a single Higher at grade C, or even a single Leadership Award, as being equivalent to those leaving school with five Higher A grades. This is despite the fact that those two pupils will quite obviously have very different post-school opportunities available to them. The government may well claim that it is 'closing the gap' amongst school leavers, but the truth is that this clumsy, broad brush approach is actually obscuring inequalities rather than highlighting them.

In 2020, I used FOI legislation to force the government to publish more detailed information about the qualification levels of school leavers. I asked them to combine data on the total number of qualifications achieved by young people with the SIMD data on pupil backgrounds, and what I found shone a new light on the inequalities lurking not just within Scottish education, but also underneath the government data. Despite claims that the attainment gap is closing, the information showed that in 2019, pupils from the richest areas were more likely to leave school with five level 6 qualifications than those from poor areas were to leave with just one. This is a staggering and wholly unacceptable divide, yet the official data published by the government simply ignores it.

And it actually gets even worse when you peel back some more of the dodgy 'one or more' varnish and get a look at what lies beneath. Following on from the investigation into the total number of qualifications achieved by school leavers from different social backgrounds, I decided to try to do the same thing around grade distributions. I wanted to find out about the chances of the poorest pupils getting an A, B, C or failing grade in their Higher exams, and to determine whether this data might reveal another of Scotland's hidden attainment gaps. It did.

In 2019, nearly 40% of all Higher awards for those from the wealthiest parts of Scotland were A grades, but in the most deprived areas that figure plummets to just 16%. In fact, pupils from the bottom half of SIMD groups were more likely to fail a Higher course than they were to get an A, while pupils from the richest parts of the country are more likely to achieve an A than any other grade. In the end, this new data makes the link between affluence and attainment brutally clear.

Exam Results: Distribution of Higher A and Fail Grades by Deprivation Level 2019

Source: Scottish Government, Freedom of Information response

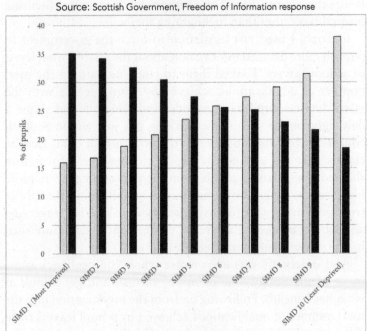

As this chart shows, there is a direct link between affluence and results: the richer a pupil is the more likely they are to be awarded an A while pupils from the bottom half of SIMD groups are more likely to fail than achieve a top grade.

In the period from 2016–2019 the data shows an 'A grade attainment gap' of more than 20 percentage points at Higher, and the divide at National 5 level is even greater. Even when we include the statistics for 2020, when the pandemic led to the cancellation of exams and an increase in overall pass rates, those gaps persisted. Full breakdowns of the 2021 results are not yet available, but the SQA's own equality monitoring report suggests that it has either remained stable or, in the case of Highers, actually increased.

It seems that no matter how results are generated within the framework of the current system, the wealthiest pupils manage to retain their advantages over others, and the poorest are still left behind. The SNP government's rhetoric has for so long focused on their promises to close these gaps – yet the data they choose to publish often seems designed to obscure, rather than illuminate, the reality for young people in Scotland. It is worth noting at this stage that all of the new information on A grade gaps and grade distributions is still government data, and the fact that it was released to me following Freedom of Information requests means that it could have been released at any time in recent years. There's no good reason why reports detailing overall pass rates, for example, shouldn't also highlight the relative figures for different social groups, but in too many cases politics has been allowed to get in the way of policy, all to the detriment of pupils.

But these poverty-related gaps are not only found in the final results of senior phase courses – they even manifest in the options available to pupils from different backgrounds. Those from the poorest parts of Scotland are not just less likely to pass their courses, and less likely to attain A grades in those that they do pass, they also have fewer choices available to them. This issue has been exacerbated by the introduction of Curriculum for Excellence, which has led to a narrowing of the curriculum in s4–6. Furthermore, research from the University of Stirling has found that the reduction in choices 'has not been uniform, but has varied between schools of different characteristics, between areas with different levels of deprivation and between local authorities'.

Exam Results: Higher and National 5 A-Grade Gap (SIMD) 2016–2020

Source: Scottish Government, Freedom of Information response

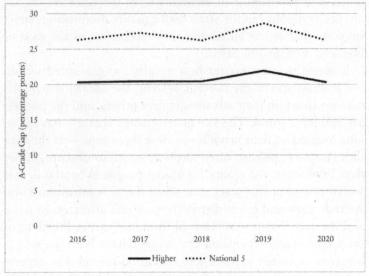

Between 2016 and 2020 the A Grade Gap between the richest and poorest pupils has barely changed.

What's more, it was found that a 'larger reduction in the number of subject entries for National 5 level qualifications took place in schools in more deprived areas, schools where the proportion of pupils with additional learning support needs was higher, and schools with poorer staff-student ratios'. This means schools serving more deprived areas are now likely to offer fewer subject choices to their pupils than schools in more affluent areas. Put simply, the poorest attempt fewer qualifications than their wealthier peers, further entrenching the gaps between the two groups.

There is still more we don't know, such as the extent to which social background has any impact on the types of subjects that pupils attempt. Even if the gap in the number of qualifications were closing, would we really be making any sort of worthwhile progress if middle-class pupils dominated the sorts of subjects associated with university access while working-class kids were funnelled towards practical areas on the assumption that this is where they belong? The official data would certainly look good – and that would no doubt be enough for some – but it wouldn't be telling us the truth.

This data on 'entries' – each individual qualification attempted by each pupil – also reveals another series of worrying divides in Scottish schooling, this time driven not by social background but by gender. Although girls are much more likely to leave school with at least one qualification at level six – 70.1% did so in 2020 compared to just 57.8% of boys – SQA statistics reveal massive and persistent gender gaps in uptake levels of a range of subjects, with boys dominating classes like physics and

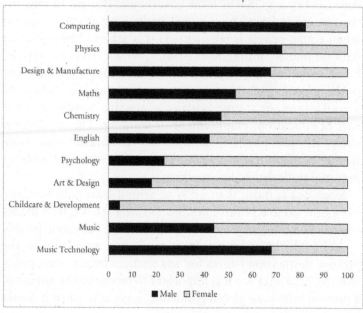

Gender Divides in Selected Higher Subject Entries 2020
Source: SQA Annual Statistical Reports

computing while girls make up the majority of students in areas like psychology and childcare. An especially striking example of the role of gender is found in the data around two connected subjects. At Higher level, girls made up nearly 60% of students in music courses, but when you add the word 'technology' and look again, you find a subject where almost 70% of students are boys.

As if the gender gaps themselves weren't bad enough, there has also been almost no progress at all in closing them over the last decade. So far, for all the talk about the need for equality, and all the money spent on developing areas such as science, technology, engineering and maths (STEM) subjects, Scotland is still a country where outdated gender expectations influence the education that our young people experience.

Positive Destinations

Another key way in which the government chooses to measure the success of Scottish schools is by looking at what happens when young people leave them. This is achieved by collecting data on pupils' 'initial destinations', which refers to 'activity being undertaken by young people three months after the end of the school year'. The ultimate goal is laudable: to have all school leavers, or at least as many as possible, heading to some sort of education, employment or training. The six specific categories for 'positive destinations' are higher education, further education, training, employment, voluntary work or personal skills development schemes.

Since 2012, more than 90% of school leavers in Scotland have gone on to a positive destination after school, with higher education comfortably the most popular route for young people.

Although the most recent stats show a small dip in the positive destination figures for 2020 school leavers – dropping from 95% to 93.3% – it is important to recognise the impact of a once-in-a-lifetime global pandemic, especially when it comes to employment opportunities for school leavers.

Unsurprisingly, this area saw the biggest fall from 2019 to 2020, dropping from 22.9% to 16.2%. The total number unemployed after leaving school increased from 4.5% to 6% – a figure that, for the record, is still an improvement on those recorded prior to 2015. Remarkably, however, the proportion of young people entering further or higher education actually increased, with the latter jumping by almost four percentage points, suggesting that even in the face of the coronavirus pandemic, the Scottish education system found ways to help

School Leaver Destinations: Initial Destinations 2020
Source: Scottish Government, Summary Stats for Attainment and Initial Leaver Destinations

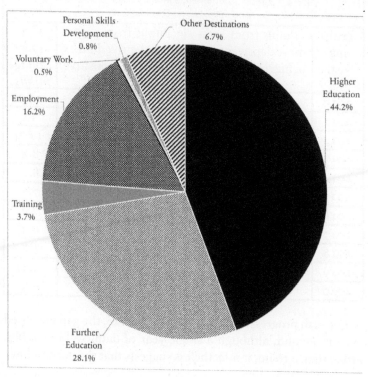

75

young people take a positive step forward upon leaving school.

The overall gap between rich and poor has also, according to the official data, more than halved since 2010. At that point, nearly a fifth of those from the most deprived parts of Scotland weren't recorded as being in a positive destination three months after leaving school, and the gap between these young people and those from the wealthiest backgrounds was 13.2 percentage points. Steady progress over the decade, however, saw that gap fall to just 5.4 percentage points in 2019, with 92.4% of those from the poorest areas securing a positive destination by this stage.

School Leaver Destinations: Positive Destinations Gap 2010–2020 Source: Scottish Government, Summary Stats for Attainment and Initial Leaver Destinations			
Leaving year	Pupils from 20% most deprived areas achieving a positive destination	Pupils from 20% least deprived areas achieving a positive destination	Gap (*percentage points*)
2010	80.4 %	93.7 %	13.2
2011	82.8 %	94.7 %	12
2012	84.1 %	95.1 %	11.1
2013	87.1 %	95.8 %	8.8
2014	88.3 %	96.5 %	8.2
2015	88.7 %	96.4 %	7.7
2016	88.9 %	96.8 %	7.9
2017	89.8 %	96.7 %	6.9
2018	90.5 %	97.3 %	6.8
2019	92.4 %	97.7 %	5.4
2020	90 %	96.3 %	6.3

But such progress is always fragile. In 2020, the gap increased once more and, although a single year of data could be a blip rather than a trend, it nonetheless suggests that the poorest have borne the brunt of reduced opportunities during the pandemic.

Even allowing for what is hopefully a one-year aberration, it is clear that some significant progress has been made, and that outcomes for school leavers, while not yet equal, are at least less unequal than ever before – but as you might expect by now, a more detailed reading of the data changes the picture, revealing significant gaps in access and opportunities.

School Leaver Destinations: Higher Education Access Gap (SIMD) 2010–2020

Source: Scottish Government, Summary Stats for Attainment and Initial Leaver Destinations

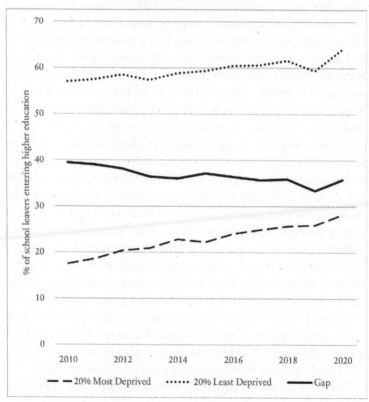

The most striking of these is found at higher education level where, even now, access is dominated by the those from the wealthiest areas. A total of 44.2% of all school leavers went on to higher education in 2020 but look behind that headline figure and we find that fewer than one third of those from the poorest areas took this route compared to nearly two thirds of those from the wealthiest postcodes. The gap between the two was just under 36 percentage points, which is barely an improvement on figures from 2010 (39.4 percentage points) and actually represents an increase compared to 2019. The poorest pupils may be more likely to go from school to higher education than they were a decade ago but, in relative terms, they are still enormously disadvantaged compared to their wealthy peers, and there is little sign of that injustice being undone any time soon.

Furthermore, an important distinction must be drawn between higher education and university access. Many people – quite reasonably – assume them to be the same thing but, in Scotland, this is not the case. Here, a significant proportion of higher education provision happens not in universities but rather in colleges, where students engage in Higher National Certificate (HNC) and Higher National Diploma (HND) courses. According to information from Colleges Scotland, the sector is responsible for 24% of all higher education provision in the country. The basic idea is that these students can then work their way onto degree courses in universities; in 2019 40% of those leavers did indeed go down this route, but large numbers of those with an HND or HNC do not have their existing learning fully recognised on entry to university. All of this leaves those particular students – who are far more likely to be from less affluent backgrounds – having to spend more time in education to reach the same point as their peers. This has serious knock-on effects, such as greater challenges for those from rural areas and a delay to the increased earnings that university graduates tend to enjoy.

There are also other problems with the imprecision of positive destinations stats. In 2017, the Scottish Government was forced to admit that it counted those on zero-hours contracts as having achieved a positive destination, despite the fact that First Minister Nicola Sturgeon had previously, and correctly, said that they 'demean and exploit' workers. In the same year, research from University College London's Institute of Education found that 'young adults who are employed on zero-hours contracts are less likely to be in good health, and are at higher risk of poor mental health than workers with stable jobs'. That doesn't sound like a particularly positive destination, but it counts as far as the official data goes.

None of this means we should dismiss the positive destinations data as entirely useless; however, we should remember that headline figures focused on absolute improvements are far less illuminating than data that highlights the trends over time and, as ever, the gaps between rich and poor.

Additional Support Needs

The government's data also allows us to examine the difference in outcomes for pupils with and without additional support needs, a cohort whose numbers have swelled significantly over the years. Factors driving individuals' additional support needs include commonly known conditions such as dyslexia, visual impairments and autistic spectrum disorders, but those with English as a second language or who have experienced interrupted learning (which is the group with the lowest percentage going on to a positive destination) are also included, as are a small number of pupils deemed to be of particularly high ability. Back in 2010, the government's pupil census recorded around 10% of pupils in Scotland's schools as having some form of additional support need; by 2020, that number had risen to more than 30%. Over that period there was an increase in all recognised ASN factors; worryingly, but perhaps unsurprisingly, the biggest jump came from pupils with mental health problems.

When looking again at 'positive destinations' data we can see that what we might call the 'ASN gap' has been falling over the last decade. In 2010 just under 80% of pupils with additional support needs went to a positive destination after school, but by 2020 the figure had risen to just under 90%. Indeed, it had exceeded 90% in both 2018 and 2019. Over most of that period, the gap between those with and without additional support needs was also heading in the right direction, falling from 8.6 percentage points in 2010 to 4.6 percentage points – the lowest ever – in 2019. We already know that the total percentage of pupils achieving positive destinations fell slightly in 2020 as the impact of the pandemic became clear, and it is grimly unsurprising to discover that those with additional needs were disproportionately affected as the gap between themselves and those without additional needs grew.

In addition to data on those with additional support needs, the government also gathers some destination information on pupils who are 'declared or assessed disabled'. It highlights a key

School Leaver Destinations: Positive Destinations Gap (ASN) 2010–2020
Source: Scottish Government, Summary Stats for Attainment and Initial Leaver Destinations

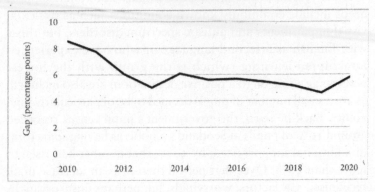

divide between those registered as having a disability and those who do not: the former are much more likely to go to college, while the latter are more likely to go to university, with very limited progress made in addressing this disparity over the last ten years. As with additional support needs, there seems to be an acceptance, even an expectation, that those with disabilities

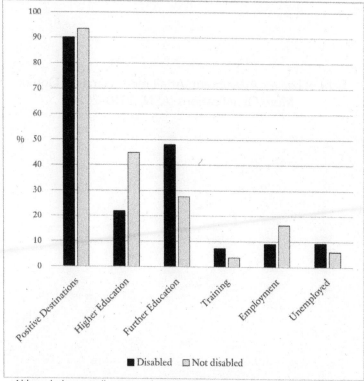

School Leaver Destinations: Initial Destinations (Disabled Students) 2020

Source: Scottish Government, Summary Stats for Attainment and Initial Leaver Destinations

Although the overall positive destinations gap is small, there are significant divides in access to higher and further education.

School Leaver Attainment: One or More Qualifications at Level 6 (ASN) 2020

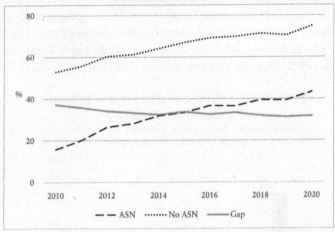

School Leaver Attainment: Attainment Gaps for One or More Qualifications (ASN) 2010–2020

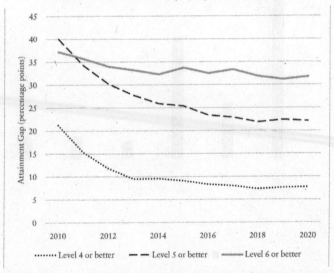

Source for graphs: Scottish Government, Summary Stats for Attainment and Initial Leaver Destinations

will just have to work harder for longer or, even worse, are just not as capable as those without disabilities.

A far wider 'ASN gap' exists, and persists, when examining the numbers leaving school with one or more qualifications at level 6. Just over 40% of young people with additional support needs achieved this in 2020, but the corresponding figure for those without additional needs was just over 75%, a gap of more than 30 percentage points. Although this does represent some progress since 2010, when the gap stood at nearly 40 percentage points, attempts to close this particular divide have been painfully slow.

Better progress has been made at levels 4 and 5, where the ASN gaps have fallen massively. Indeed, the patterns of improvement for levels 4 and 5 are very similar, which makes the progress, or lack thereof, at level 6 over the same period particularly striking. Why should pupils with additional support needs be at such a disadvantage when it comes to this key metric of the education system, and what does it say about the system and structures in place that we seem, thus far, to be largely powerless to do anything about it? If these are young people who need additional support, then this data suggests that we are failing to provide it. What's more, the latest data shows that pupils recorded as being in special schools or in mainstream schools with additional support needs are significantly more likely to come from the most deprived areas than the most affluent, confirming that these divides are also a class issue.

Urban vs Rural

We already know that SIMD and Free School Meals data allows us to break down performance and understand some of the gaps between different groups and different schools, but it is also possible to consider the influence of the types of places that pupils live.

One of the Scottish Government's lesser-known data sets

analyses the country according to something called the Urban Rural Classification system, using population and accessibility data to rate every settlement in Scotland as either urban or rural and accessible or remote. The main focus of the data has six sections, although another two categories are also available.

The Scottish Government combines this information with some of the more common metrics, such as literacy levels and leaver data, meaning that it is possible to get a glimpse of Scotland's geographical attainment gap.

School Leaver Attainment: One or More Qualifications at Level 6 (Urban Rural) 2010–2020
Source: Scottish Government, Summary Stats for Attainment and Initial Leaver Destinations

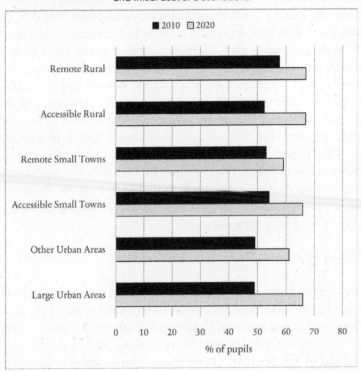

Urban Rural Classification System		
Category	Specifications	Examples
Large urban area	Settlements of 125,000 people and over.	Glasgow, Edinburgh, Aberdeen, Dundee
Other urban area	Settlements of 10,000 to 124,999 people.	Ayr, Cumbernauld, Fort William, Kirkintilloch, Stonehaven
Accessible small town	Settlements of 3,000 to 9,999 people, and within a 30 minute drive time of a settlement of 10,000 or more.	Beith, Garelochhead, Jedburgh, Stewarton, Wemyss Bay
Remote small town	Settlements of 3,000 to 9,999 people, and with a drive time of over 30 minutes to a settlement of 10,000 or more.	Aviemore, Dingwall, Girvan, Kirkcudbright, Macduff
Very remote small town	*Settlements of 3,000 to 9,999 people, and with a drive time of over 60 minutes to a Settlement of 10,000 or more.*	*Campbeltown, Dunoon, Kirkwall, Oban, Tain*
Accessible rural area	Areas with a population of less than 3,000 people, and within a drive time of 30 minutes to a settlement of 10,000 or more.	Aberlour, Croy, Fochabers, Lochwinnoch, Portpatrick
Remote rural area	Areas with a population of less than 3,000 people, and with a drive time of over 30 minutes to a settlement of 10,000 or more.	Creetown, Fortrose, Millport, Pitlochry, Sanquhar,
Very remote rural area	*Areas with a population of less than 3,000 people, and with a drive time of over 60 minutes to a settlement of 10,000 or more.*	*Brora, Lamlash, Lochgilphead, Mallaig, Ullapool*

When you analyse the data there seems to be a clear issue with pupils in remote parts of the country: across every stage of primary school (primary 1, primary 4, primary 7 and primary 1, 4 & 7 combined) and according to every metric (reading, writing, listening and talking, overall literacy and overall numeracy) they are less likely to achieve the expected curricular level for their age. Those in areas classified as remote are up to 14 percentage points behind children in other parts of Scotland when it comes to literacy, while in numeracy the gap is 12 points. In secondary school those from remote rural areas largely catch up with, and even surpass, their peers from urban and accessible areas, but those from remote small towns continue to lag behind in terms of literacy and numeracy.

Divides can also be found when examining school leaver data broken down by the 6-fold Urban Rural Classification system. In 2020, 47.4% of leavers from Scotland's large urban areas went on to higher education, but for young people from remote small towns that figure is just 36.9%. Those from remote areas are significantly more likely to go straight into employment after school than students from other parts of Scotland. In terms of attainment statistics, these show that fewer than 60% of leavers from remote small towns have at least one qualification at level six, once again the lowest of all six categories. What is especially striking is that while the performance of pupils from urban areas (which people might typically expect to record the worst results) has significantly improved over the last decade, those from remote small towns seem to have been left behind.

It is not immediately clear why living in remote areas, especially remote small towns, would have such a persistent impact on pupil attainment and post-school destinations. Schools in remote areas often find it harder to recruit teachers, which seems likely to have an effect, but other factors – such as a lack of transport links suppressing wages by limiting opportunities for those without cars – could also come into play. How many school leavers in these areas didn't go to college or university because, for example, they could neither afford to commute every day or to move house. This all serves as a useful reminder that the issues that manifest in school data are often more likely to be addressed by examining social and geographical rather than strictly educational factors.

Care Experienced Young People

One of the most shameful aspects of the Scottish education system is the way in which it fails young people with experience of the care system. As ever, examples of structural progress can be found if that's what you go searching for, but those scattered forward steps can all-too-easily be used to mask the continuing and

School Leaver Attainment: Positive Destination Rates (Care Experienced) 2010–2019

Source: Scottish Government, Looked after children education outcomes

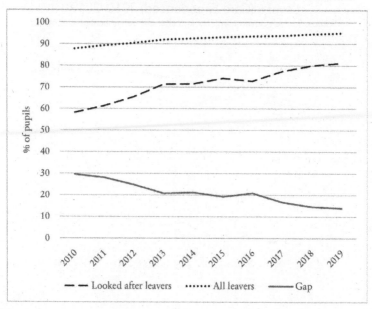

unacceptable realities for far too many young people in Scotland.

In 2010, just under 60% of young people with experience of the care system went on to a positive destination after school. By 2019 this number had massively improved, with more than 80% going on to some form of education, training or employment. An increase of more than 20 percentage points over a decade should certainly be recognised, as should the fact that the gap between care experienced young people and the population as a whole has more than halved over the same period. There's no doubt that things are better than they were, and considerably so.

But what happens if we dig beyond the headline figures and look in greater detail at attainment levels and post-school destinations of care experienced young people?

Let's start by examining one of the government's main – albeit flawed – measurements: achieving one or more qualifications

School Leaver Attainment: One or More Qualifications at Level 6 (Care Experienced) 2010–2019

Source: Scottish Government, Looked after children education outcomes

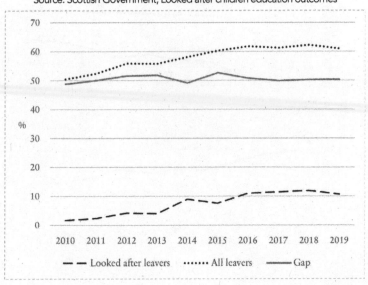

at level 6. In 2019, just over 60% of school leavers overall had managed to achieve this relatively modest goal; the equivalent figure for those with care experience was just 10.6%, a gap of more than 50 percentage points. That gap is actually slightly larger than it was a decade ago, when it stood at 48.8 percentage points and fewer than 2% of care experienced school leavers had a level 6 qualification.

So, by some measures progress has been made, but in relative terms – which are actually more important in this sort of context – we seem to have gotten nowhere over the last decade.

At the level below things are little better. Nearly 35% of care experienced school leavers in 2019 had at least one level 5 qualification, but with the figure for the whole population standing at 85.4% the gap between the two is actually marginally greater than at level 6. It has, at least, declined over the last ten years, but that is scant consolation in the face of divides that are not so much gaps as yawning chasms, and which still mean that even today two thirds of care experienced young people leave school without even a single National 5 or equivalent. In fact, nearly a fifth of those with experience of the care system leave school without a single qualification at even level 3 or above, while the corresponding figure for the total pupil population is just 2%.

And it is much the same story when we look into the details of school leavers' destinations, particularly access to higher education. Back in 2010 more than 36% of all school leavers went straight to higher education, but just 1% of care experienced young people did so; today those figures stand at 40.3% and 5.2%. The gap has closed by a grand total of 0.1 percentage points. More than four in ten care experienced young people go to further education straight after school, and from here may go on to higher education, but that still leaves them having to overcome more barriers and spend more time just to reach the same point as their peers, all because of circumstances entirely outwith their own control. This sort of divide could

School Leaver Attainment: Higher Education Access Rates (Care Experienced) 2010–2019

Source: Scottish Government, Looked after children education outcomes

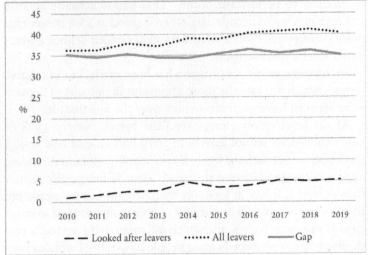

only be tolerable if you believed that young people in care are simply and inherently uninterested in, or ill-suited for, higher education; otherwise, it is an outrage.

All too often a lack of understanding and flexibility from the school system, or continuity and consideration from the care system, as well as the persistent social stigma that surrounds them, leaves these young people disrespected, alienated and held back. Recently we have seen greater attention than ever before being paid to care experienced young people. The national plan known as The Promise states that, by 2024, they will 'receive all they need to thrive at school' and that there will be 'no barriers to their engagement with education'. If that promise is to be kept, and care experienced young people really are to be 'able to realise their full potential', then unprecedented progress will be required over the coming years.

5

A Crisis in Our Classrooms?

ALTHOUGH WE NEED to be realistic about what schools can achieve in the face of persistent, deep-seated and enormously destructive social inequalities, that doesn't mean that the education system is entirely powerless.

Teachers can and do have a huge and positive impact on the lives of their students, but their capacity for changing lives is dependent upon the environment in which they are operating. Class sizes, teacher numbers, workload, support levels and even the demographics of the workforce all matter, and greater understanding is required of how these factors interact with issues such as inequality and discrimination. After all, teachers' working conditions are students' learning conditions, so if we want to give our children the best possible start, we need to give our teachers the support they deserve.

Class Sizes

In its manifesto for the 2007 Holyrood election the SNP made a specific and memorable promise about schools: they pledged that they would deliver 'smaller class sizes, starting with a reduction in the first three years of primary to 18 or less'. They argued that such a move would give pupils in primary 1, primary 2 and primary 3 'more time with their teacher at this vital stage of their development' and, somewhat bizarrely even for a manifesto, claimed that this shift would also 'help tackle indiscipline in schools'.

As pretty much everyone knows, the party never came close to fulfilling this promise to Scotland's youngest pupils. By the time of the 2011 election, the SNP made no mention of the '18 or less' pledge, instead promising 'a new legal limit of 25 on class sizes in primary 1'. Class sizes weren't mentioned at all in the 2016 or 2021 manifestos. The closest the party ever came to meeting its target was in 2010, when just over a fifth of primary 1–3 pupils were being taught in classes of 18 of fewer, but by 2014 this number had dropped down to just under 13%, which is almost exactly where it had been the year before the SNP took power.

Even the most recent statistics, published in December 2020, show that the average class sizes for pupils in primary 1, primary 2 and primary 3 are 21, 24 and 24 respectively and that just 14% of primary 1–3 pupils are being taught in classes of 18

School Statistics: Distribution of Primary 1–3 Pupils by Class Size 2020
Source: Scottish Government, Schools in Scotland 2020

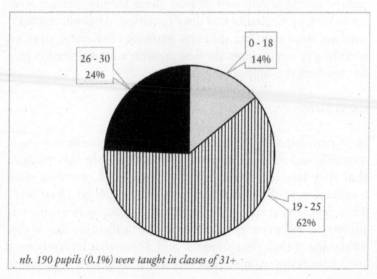

26 - 30
24%

0 - 18
14%

19 - 25
62%

nb. 190 pupils (0.1%) were taught in classes of 31+

or fewer. Today, the truth is that the overwhelming majority of the youngest pupils are taught in classes of 19–25, and there are more in classes of 26 and above than there are in classes of 18 or fewer.

No matter how you cut it, when it comes to class sizes in Scottish schools successive SNP governments have failed miserably, and it's not just the youngest pupils who have lost out as a result. That original manifesto promise said that smaller classes in primary 1–3 would be the starting point, implying that class sizes across primary 4–7 would then be brought down as well. Unsurprisingly, this hasn't happened either: in 2007 the average class size for primary school pupils was 23.2; today it stands at 23.1.

Smaller classes isn't a silver bullet and needs to be partnered with other policy changes including a reorganisation of teachers' time. That said, there's simply no getting away from the fact that with fewer students in the class it is easier to, for example, give each one detailed and rapid feedback to help them improve. Pupils are more likely to feel like they are noticed by their teacher, which should help with the quality of their work and the pace of their progress. Fewer jotters to mark also means that teachers have more time to plan high-quality lessons that meet the developing needs of the young people in their classes. Marginal reductions are unlikely to have significant impacts on classroom culture or young people's attainment, but the bigger the drop the greater the potential for improvement. It's not difficult to see why all this would be particularly important with children aged between four and seven years old, but it applies across the board.

Unfortunately, official data on class sizes is almost entirely limited to primary schools because measuring it in high schools is so much more complicated. In primary, pupils are in a single, settled class throughout the year, but secondary pupils see several teachers per day, may not see all of them every week, and, by fourth year, aren't all doing the same subjects, making any overall comparisons largely impossible.

So we know, for example, that the pupil-teacher ratio across all secondary schools in 2020 was 12.5, but this is simply the number you get when you divide the total number of secondary pupils that year (300,954) by the total number of secondary teachers (24,077). The secondary pupil-teacher ratio is also remarkably consistent across the country. The three island authorities of Orkney, Shetland and Na h-Eileanan Siar have the lowest ratios due to very low pupil numbers, but once they are excluded the figures range from a low of 11.15 pupils per teacher in Argyll & Bute to a high of 13.57 in Fife. But of course, these simple numbers could be hiding large variations between schools or even within them, and anything but enormous variations from year to year wouldn't necessarily tell us much of value at a national level.

That being the case, perhaps it would be better to think about high school class sizes in terms of the difference between so-called practical subjects and the rest, the implications this has for overall class sizes, and what sort of changes could be beneficial?

In high schools, classes in S1 and S2 are limited to 33 pupils, with an at least theoretical upper limit of 30 for S3–S6 classes. A cap of 20 pupils is applied in subjects such as sciences, hospitality, woodworking and others, and this limit is typically regarded as important for pupil safety. There are, however, inconsistencies in the list of subjects to which this rule applies: administration and IT, for example, is included in the list, while computing science is not, and although the inclusion of art is ultimately justified because it is a subject in which students 'do things', the same consideration is not extended to music or, incredibly, PE

But all of this begs an obvious question: to what extent would universal class size limits of 20 improve young people's experience of school? If it benefits students to ensure that a physics teacher has no more than 20 pupils in the room at any one time, then why wouldn't the same be true in a maths or Spanish class, or in primary schools? Even where Bunsen burners and frying pans and table saws aren't part of day-to-day learning, the principle remains the same in any classroom: fewer pupils allows the teacher to give more attention to each individual. Although the government may have turned its focus away class sizes (in so small part because of issues with teacher numbers that are explored next) but it is nonetheless one of the key factors that could be addressed in order to improve education in Scotland.

Teacher Numbers

Obviously, reducing class sizes depends on a critical factor: the number of available teachers. This, however, is another area that the SNP have found particularly challenging over the years. In 2007, while making promises they couldn't keep on primary school class sizes, the SNP also pledged to 'maintain teacher numbers in the face of falling school rolls'. It didn't happen. When the SNP came to power there were 50,402 teachers in Scotland's primary and secondary schools; in 2014, after year-on-year declines, that number had dipped to 46,361. Since then, the numbers have gradually increased each year, and by 2020 reached a total of 49,728, an overall loss of 674.

But the changes were not spread evenly across all schools: while the number of teachers in secondary schools dropped by almost 2,500 between 2007 and 2020, the number of primary teachers has actually increased by more than 1,800 in the same period (although so have pupil numbers in primary schools).

There are also teachers who do not work in primary or secondary schools, although the numbers are fairly small and the specifics of the job sometimes quite distinct from a standard classroom teacher role. They are, nonetheless, a vital part of the school system and their numbers need to be considered too.

School Statistics: Teacher Numbers (Primary and Secondary Schools) 2007–2020
Source: Scottish Government, Schools in Scotland 2020

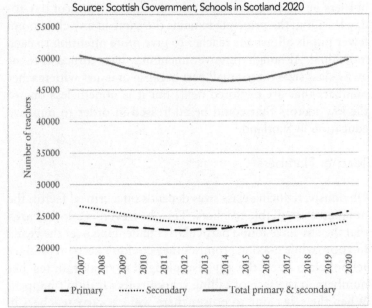

The number of teachers in special schools has fallen from 2,044 in 2007 to 1,934 now, having bottomed out at 1,836 in 2017. Though some may assume that this dip can be explained by falling pupil numbers, with more and more young people moved from special schools to mainstream settings, the data doesn't back up such an assertion. In 2007 there were 6,709 pupils at 183 special schools across Scotland, whereas in 2020 there were 7,286 pupils in 114 special schools. Some 'efficiencies' would appear to have been found through the reduction in the number of special schools, but that presumably means the people attending them now also face bigger classes. In Scotland we also have a small number of teachers, such as specialists working between different schools, who are counted as being 'centrally employed'. Their numbers have varied significantly over the last decade, going from 714 in 2010 to a high of 1,283 in 2015 and now standing at 1,009.

The overall pattern is unmistakable. In 2007, the grand total for all teachers in Scotland's publicly funded schools system stood at 53,411, a number which declined every year until 2014 (49,521) before starting to recover. The latest figure is 52,672, which is a loss of 739 teachers over the full period of SNP control of the Scottish Government. After 14 years in power, and with education allegedly their number one priority (at least for a while), the SNP haven't even been able to restore the teacher numbers that they inherited.

Falling teacher numbers cause an obvious problem with class sizes but it doesn't end there. Schools with fewer teaching staff also have less capacity overall, so those teachers who do remain might spend more of their planning and marking time covering absences or find it increasingly difficult to gain permission to attend important training and development sessions. It also becomes more challenging to provide things like extra-curricular activities for young people. Schools, like anything else, simply do not work as well when they are constantly being pushed to their operational limits.

The Scottish Government would naturally defend itself by pointing out that it does not employ teachers or run schools – instead, this responsibility lies with individual councils. Surely, then, criticism around teacher numbers should be directed towards local, not national, government? This is true, up to a point, but the argument is fatally undermined by the fact that the overwhelming majority of council budgets come from central government grants, and that those funding levels have been cut more severely than the overall reductions faced by the government itself. Councils have also been prevented from raising more funds themselves.

Furthermore, a political party that chases votes by making manifesto pledges about teacher numbers cannot then complain when people try to hold them to account. In its 2021 manifesto, the SNP promised to recruit a further (combined) 3,500 teachers and classroom assistants, and following their election victory they specified that this would begin with 1,000 more teachers and 500 more classroom assistants 'within the first 100 days' of the new parliamentary term. Applying this ratio to the originally promised total suggests an eventual increase of roughly 2,300 teachers and 1,200 support staff, which would leave the country with around 1,600 more teachers than we had in 2007. In statistical terms, that represents an increase of less than 3% over 15 years.

Of course, all of this assumes that this latest promise about teacher numbers is actually going to be delivered, but it might be better to believe that when we see it.

Experienced Staff

While attracting enthusiastic, high-quality new teachers is extremely important, another serious issue in Scottish schools has been the extraordinary rate at which we have lost experienced teachers over the past ten years.

In 2010, the average age of the teaching profession in Scotland was 43 years old; by 2020, this has dropped to 40 years old. This might not seem like much of a change at first but, as the chart below shows, it is part of a significant shift in the overall age profile of the workforce.

Analysing the more detailed age breakdowns makes things even clearer. A decade ago, half of Scotland's teachers were aged 45 or over, which is typically old enough to have been in the profession for 20 years; today, only 37% of those teaching in Scotland's schools possess that level of experience. This loss has been felt in primary, secondary and special schools, as well as amongst those who are centrally employed.

These declines mean that the overall age distribution of

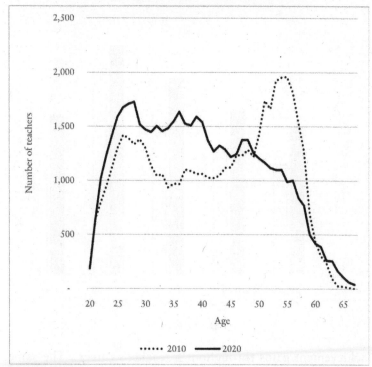

School Statistics: Age Distribution of the Teaching Workforce 2010–2020
Source: Scottish Government, Schools in Scotland 2020

•••••• 2010 ———— 2020

the profession has shifted dramatically towards younger, less-experienced educators. The issue has been largely ignored and, even when it has been noticed, has been presented as an example of progress by some, as if pulling down the average age of a profession is automatically, for whatever reason, a good idea – but what if that isn't actually true?

For one thing, there is plenty of evidence to suggest that teachers become more effective as they become more experienced. A 2016 report by the Learning Policy Institute in the USA found that 'teaching experience is positively associated with student

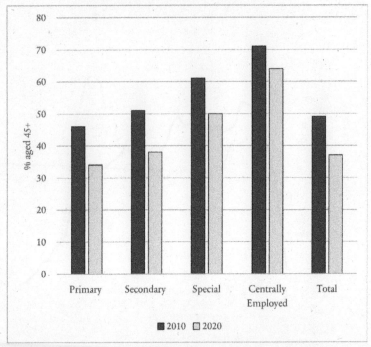

School Statistics: Percentage of the Teaching Workforce Aged 45+ by Sector 2010–2020
Source: Scottish Government, Schools in Scotland 2020

achievement gains throughout a teacher's career'. The same report suggested that the benefits are not just restricted to test scores, with improvements in areas such as school attendance also highlighted. Furthermore, the presence of experienced teachers also seems to 'support greater student learning for their colleagues and the school as a whole'. So, they don't just help their own students, but in fact benefit all students.

This really shouldn't be a surprise when we think about it logically. In the early stages of their careers, teachers are expected to rapidly develop their knowledge and skills in a wide range of areas: it's not just about *knowing* what you're meant to be teaching, but also getting better and better at identifying the *best ways* of teaching it in a variety of different contexts and for students with a wide range of abilities, motivation levels and outside experiences. The job is incredibly complex, demanding the constant reassessment of hundreds of moving parts, and it takes a long time and a huge amount of work to get really, really good at it – in a system like Scotland's, where teachers are seriously overworked and still under-appreciated, it is even more difficult.

Those who have been doing the job for 20 years or more, learning and developing along the way, and supporting new teachers during their initial steps into the profession, have an immense wealth of knowledge, skills and expertise to tap into, but they also have the benefit of having outlasted numerous new initiatives, education secretaries and governments.

I've seen the value of this first-hand as a brand new teacher at Arran High School. My head of department, Alan Kelly, had been teaching for nearly 30 years when I met him. He taught me the actual mechanics of real-world teaching, but more than that he taught me how to focus on what really matters. Almost all paperwork, he used to tell me, should be ignored the first time it appears – if it *actually* matters someone will ask for it a second time. He literally laughed at me when I asked him if I should spend time writing out lessons plans for him to check over, and instead told me that I should never be trying to make detailed plans more than a week or so in advance, because that meant I was concentrating on what I wanted rather than what my students needed.

But the most important piece of advice he ever gave me, and without doubt the best advice I ever received as a teacher, was simple: ignore all the gimmicks and '*just teach the weans*'.

He was right. In education there's no end to consultants with flashy new ideas, or the ladder-climbers talking up their short-term cv-building projects, or salespeople punting the latest game-changing tech – but the focus, always, forever, and above all else, should be the pupils. Alan had been in the job long enough to see an endless parade of 'next big things' and whole curriculums come and go, and in all that time the thing that had remained constant was the simple truth that teaching is about helping young people. Lose sight of that and you lose sight of everything.

None of which is to say that young teachers, with all that energy and enthusiasm, and the ability to bring new ideas and approaches and perspectives into the profession, aren't valuable – they're vital. At 34 years old I'd probably be considered a youngster by many of the teachers for whom I have the most respect, and I think that, all things considered, I was a good teacher while I was lucky enough to work on Arran in my mid-20s, but I'm not convinced that would have been the case had I not been supported by brilliant and experienced teachers across the school and, indeed, across the country. It's about balance.

So, what is driving this obvious and worrying demographic change in the teaching profession? I reported on these trends for *The Herald* a few years ago – when they were beginning to emerge but not yet fully apparent – and was told that while a great deal of emphasis was being placed on recruiting new teachers, not enough was being done to hold on to those we already had. A combination of ever-increasing workloads, limited opportunities for development, ongoing problems with Curriculum for Excellence and an intangible change in culture were pushing experienced teachers out of a profession that they had loved. The situation does not appear to have improved.

But don't just take my word for it – listen to two of those who have recently left the profession.

I had a few reasons for leaving teaching early.

Having led a big English department for nearly 15 years I had taken them through the updated Higher courses, the new

Intermediate courses and then the implementation of CfE. The latter was like trying to nail jelly to the ceiling trying to get clear guidance on what it actually was, what help and assistance was available, and what standards and expectations it had.

There was the constant demand to 'improve' dictated to schools by politicians who showed little to no understanding of school life; the lack of quality in the leaders in Education Scotland and SQA (the latter group just seemed to be led by administrators who did not seem to have any concept of the impact of their drive to meet admin targets); the exhausting demands by some parents who seemed to think if their child struggled teachers would always find a solution; the constant monitoring of pupils' work as some parents were quite happy to cheat the system.

We were also coping with the cuts year-on-year from 2007 which resulted in a lack of staff and resources, and managing the resulting stress for teachers asked to do more and more. Then came changes to timetables, with local authorities squeezing more and more classes into the timetable. 30 in Higher was the norm and the volume of work that entailed was a huge problem.

All of the above you can cope with when young but it eventually takes its toll and burns out your enthusiasm and love of the job. I loved my job but found near the end it was like finding you don't love someone anymore and no matter how hard you try, you cannot get that love back. I was heartbroken at that and knew I could not keep going. When you lose enthusiasm and love of teaching you start to feel angry and can become cynical and I did not want to be that type of teacher. I was lucky enough that I could leave. I don't know the toll it would have taken on my mental health if I'd had to keep going.

For 90% of my career I thought I had the best job in the world but in those final years the feeling that your best was never good enough was just too exhausting to bear.

***

There was a time when being a classroom teacher was the thing to be. The reverence of the job, the craft of teaching was something to which we could aspire. When I first started 20-odd years ago, there was time for team teaching, for developing resources together as a department, for getting out of school for self-selected CPD events. To stay in the classroom was a goal for some, admirable, something to be proud of. And, regardless of how the Chartered Teacher scheme turned out, the profession seemed to think so to.

Rewarding teachers for extending knowledge of classroom practice was a laudable goal. I don't know what changed. It may or may not have been the transformation into CfE but, as someone who was a PGDE mentor, I began to notice that younger teachers were coming in with different dreams. The era of CfE produced new roles in PEF, Health and Wellbeing, Developing Young Workforce, and a whole rake of PT jobs suddenly became available. Pupil Support departments exploded in size and career pathways were opened up. Younger teachers could become PTs of something or other within three years of starting, sometimes earlier. Perhaps it was a culture of managerialism in the country in general that meant promotion was all. If you weren't looking to move 'upwards' then you probably lacked ambition and shouldn't be taken too seriously.

So what we got was an increasingly dominant middle management with little classroom experience. And God love them. The kids certainly love them. Of course, they do. Never having taught a full cycle – that is, watching an S1 pupil grow up through to S6 – never having learned the challenges and heartaches, the joy and the tears, of teaching kids through all the years. Making decisions about children with such a lack of experience – nice people though they usually are – just seems misguided to me. The hugely important areas of health and wellbeing etc seems to have taken a more important role than your actual teaching. And, even in the short term, that concerns me.

I'm leaving teaching for mostly positive reasons: 22 years

seems to be enough for me. I'm still young enough to do all of those things that I never had time for and fortunate enough to have the money to do so. I'll have no bitterness or no regrets: I'll avoid being the grumpy guy who moans about everything. But I recognise how that happens to people now. Classroom teachers are generally marginalised from any serious decision-making. We're over-stretched and exhausted. I can't remember the last time I really enjoyed teaching purely for the sake of it, to be able to plan creative and imaginative lessons without having to give up Sundays and every evening. I'll certainly miss the classroom, but I won't miss any of the meaningless managerialism that goes with it. It's a wonderful job but there is a great danger that it becomes a deskilled and thankless task.

Gender Gaps

Yet another area deserving of attention is the gender balance – or rather the lack of it – in the teaching profession. That teaching is dominated by women should not be news to anyone, but national data still reveals specific and concerning details.

In total, more than three quarters of Scotland's working teachers are women, but this gender divide is not evenly distributed across different sectors. At primary level, only 11% of teachers are men yet in secondary schools this figure jumps to 36%. Fewer than a quarter of teachers in special schools are men, and the number falls even further amongst the 1,000-or-so teachers who are centrally employed.

These numbers have barely changed in the last decade and raise some difficult questions, not just for schools but for society as a whole: can these large gender gaps, particularly that chasm at primary level, tell us something about perceptions of the teaching profession amongst men, or assumptions about men who choose to work with young children? What sort of impact might these disparities have on the experiences of children, or

School Statistics: Gender Distribution of the Teaching Workforce 2020

Source: Scottish Government, Schools in Scotland 2020

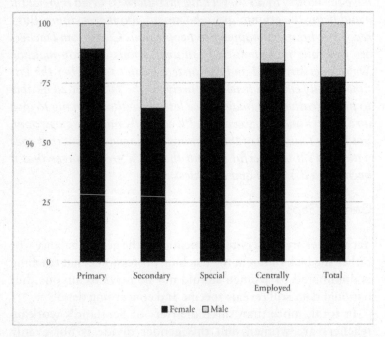

their perceptions about the roles of men and women in society?

A further gender divide can be found in the types of contracts under which teachers are working. 20% of teachers in primary schools work part-time, but 95% of that group are women; the same proportion of primary teachers are on temporary contracts, with women making up 88% of that number. The picture is slightly better in secondary schools, where women make up 85% of part-time teachers and just under two thirds of those on temporary contracts.

There are even more questions when we look past the overall figures and concentrate on those actually running schools rather than simply teaching in them.

In primary schools, the 89% female workforce is represented fairly well in promoted posts, with 84% of headteachers and 87% of both depute heads and principal teachers being women. In secondaries, however, there is clearly a problem: the workforce is 64% female, and women make up 63% of principal teachers and 58% of depute heads – but only 42 percent of headteachers. Although most of Scotland's high school classrooms are run by women, most of the top jobs in those same schools are held by men.

So, while an increase in male teachers across the profession is certainly desirable, particular attention also needs to be paid to the gender balance of management roles, especially in high schools.

Ethnic Diversity

Alongside data on characteristics such as age and gender, the Scottish Government also collects and publishes information on the ethnicity of those teaching in our schools. The overwhelming majority of Scotland's teachers are white, which is hardly surprising, but the specific data on those recorded as being from a 'minority ethnic group' suggests that the teaching profession is lacking in diversity when compared to the country as a whole.

In the 2011 Scottish census, four percent of the total Scottish population was recorded as being from a minority ethnic group, double the proportion from a decade earlier. The next national census in Scotland is due to be held in 2022, having been delayed by a year due to the coronavirus pandemic, and one would hope that the country has become even more diverse over the last eleven years; however, up-to-date census data already exists for school pupils and shows that only 89% of them are categorised as white. In contrast, however, just 1% of primary teachers, 2% of secondary teachers and two percent of special school teachers in Scotland are currently recorded as being from a minority ethnic group. The outlier is centrally employed teachers, where a whole 5% are from minority ethnic groups, although this cohort represents less than 2% of all teachers in the country.

Things are even worse when we once again examine leadership positions rather than overall teacher numbers. According to the Scottish Government's 2020 teacher census, there are seven primary school headteachers and nine depute headteachers (0.4% and 0.6% of the respective totals) from minority ethnic groups; in secondary schools, the figures are not even provided because both numbers are lower than five.

The disparities are bad enough at a national level, but they are further magnified in some specific areas. Glasgow is Scotland's most diverse city and around a quarter of pupils come from minority ethnic groups, but the same is true for just 3% of primary teachers and 5% of secondary teachers. Non-white people make up 10% of secondary pupils in Dundee but account for just 2% of secondary school teachers. In Edinburgh, only 2% of primary teachers are non-white compared with a figure of 20% for their pupils. In all but two council areas the number of minority ethnic teachers in special schools is less than five.

According to a report for the Coalition for Racial Equality and Rights (CRER) there is only one council area in Scotland where those from minority ethnic groups make up more than 4% of the teaching population. The same report points out that 'BME groups are over-represented in teaching applications, but under-represented in shortlisted candidates, appointed candidates, and staff in post'. Given the role teachers play in the lives of children this situation should be a serious cause for concern, yet it is barely discussed during debates about the state of schooling in Scotland. In 2018, a ground-breaking report entitled *Teaching in a Diverse Scotland: Increasing and Retaining Minority Ethnic Teachers in Scotland's Schools* made a total of 17 detailed and demanding recommendations for change across five key themes:

- Closing the awareness gap
- Attractiveness and status of teaching to students from minority ethnic backgrounds
- Effectiveness of university admissions processes in capturing a diverse range of applicants
- Student placement experiences and support for students
- Retaining student teachers and teachers from minority ethnic backgrounds and supporting their promotion at all levels.

The suggested changes include recognising the value of multilingual teachers, providing powerful anti-racist resources for schools, gathering better data about minority ethnic students' applications to and graduation from teaching courses, and ensuring that organisations running Scottish education include space for minority ethnic teachers.

In her foreword the report, Professor Rowena Arshad highlights exactly why all of this matters so much:

> Some might argue that the demographics of the teaching workforce should not matter and what really counts is the quality of individual teachers. Our work does not question that young people are being well served by the Scottish teaching profession. However, the words of a young person I spoke with as part of my research on race equality matters rings out for me: 'If I cannot see myself there, then I cannot imagine myself there'.

Too many pupils in Scotland go through their entire time at school without ever being able to see themselves in their teachers, and the lack of diversity in the profession also means that we are failing to take full advantage of the wealth of knowledge and experience that is available in our society. Tackling this issue must become a priority.

Support Staff

The size and composition of the teaching profession is clearly a crucial aspect of the education system, but support staff also play a critical role in schools. Unfortunately, the available data on this section of the workforce makes it incredibly difficult to establish a clear picture of what is going on across the country.

The currently published data shows a continuous increase in the number of pupil support assistants between 2017 and 2020, with the most recent figure being 15,263 full-time equivalent staff members. This represents the total number working in primary, secondary and special schools as well as those centrally employed. The figures only go back to 2017, however, because that is when the Scottish Government changed the way in which it reported support staff numbers, reducing the amount of detail available in its official publications. The new approach includes significant caveats, including a warning of 'major issues' with calculating the appropriate categorisation, as well as the funding and employment status, of those recorded as behaviour support or home school link workers. There are also 'minor issues' with the data around library staff and pupil support assistants, the latter by far the biggest group. The only category with no known issues in the national data is educational psychologists, of which there are 378 across Scotland's nearly 2,500 schools – one for every 1,858 pupils.

The pupil support assistant category is further complicated by the fact that it actually combines general classroom assistants with care assistants and additional support needs auxiliaries, and to make matters even more confusing many councils do not even use those terms, referring instead to pupil support officers or learning assistants. This imprecision means that, for example, a reduction in specialist ASN staff (the type who might be responsible for a feeding tube or medication) could be hidden by an increase in the number of general classroom assistants, which would have a major impact on schools, and damage the experiences of pupils, but would not be picked up by official data. Prior to 2017 the government's annual schools census also included much more detailed breakdowns of the variety of support staff in Scotland's schools, including specific numbers of admin and clerical staff, laboratory assistants, technicians, foreign language assistants and many more. All of that detail now seems to have been stripped from the government's official publications.

The numerous issues with the data, whether it be the change in methodology a few years ago or the variations in reporting, make it extremely difficult to make accurate, year-on-year comparisons. However, a 2017 report by Unison Scotland found that there were at that stage 1,841 fewer support staff in schools than had been the case in 2010, and that more than half reported falling budgets and low morale. The last few years have, then, seen an apparent increase in the number of at least some support staff in classrooms across Scotland, but this comes after a period of severe cuts and excessive workloads. What's more, the quality of information now available to us seems to have been reduced, making it harder than ever to uncover the truth, hold our leaders to account, or ensure that we are doing the best we can for young people in schools.

6

Coping With Covid

IN DECEMBER 2019, the first cases of Covid-19 were identified in Wuhan, China. In the weeks that followed, the virus that causes the disease was identified but also began to spread across the world: the first case outside of China was reported in Thailand on the 13th of January, and the UK saw its first infections just over a fortnight later. The World Health Organisation officially declared a global health emergency at the end of January 2020 and then, on the 11th of March, confirmed that we were officially living through a pandemic.

The First School Closures and 2020 Results Scandal

On Thursday the 19th of March, the Scottish Government announced that schools would close at the end of the following day. Hospitality businesses were also closed and everyone was encouraged to work from home; within a few days, a 'stay at home' order had been issued. With the exception of 'hubs' established to accommodate vulnerable young people and the children of key workers, schools would not physically reopen until after the summer holidays.

The emergency naturally proved an enormous challenge for teachers, parents and pupils. Schools were expected to continue offering some sort of educational provision to young people but, with no time to plan the transition and limited existing use of remote learning technologies, outcomes varied from area to area, school to school and even teacher to teacher. Obvious problems such as unequal access to technology could be magnified by the need for everyone to be using devices at the same time. Parents were understandably concerned about the impact of school closures on their children, and many felt under pressure to create classroom-like experiences at home, followed by tremendous anxiety and guilt when this proved impossible. The lack of an easily accessible set of national resources was contrasted with projects like the Oak Academy in England, which was given millions of pounds of funding to produce thousands of online lesson materials. Young people lost their daily routine and, probably worst of all, face-to-face contact with their friends, and discussions increasingly turned towards the impact of this experience on their social development and mental health. Many parents worried about widely reported disparities in things such as the use of video calls between teachers and pupils. As ever, it quickly became clear that those from the most deprived backgrounds would also be facing the greatest barriers.

Although teachers did the best they could to remain connected with their pupils, the circumstances were, by definition, extraordinary. Some teachers (and lots of young people) faced significant barriers, from a lack of experience in using online platforms to insufficiently reliable internet access to do so at home. They might be able to send out workbooks and activities to pupils, but making that work supportive for some, challenging for others and meaningful for all, without ever being in the same room as the pupils completing it, is incredibly difficult. Many teachers were also looking after their own children while trying to find ways to offer at least some learning to their classes. Nonetheless, school staff across Scotland worked incredibly hard during the first lockdown, doing all they could to support the young people to whom they are so dedicated, and they should be incredibly proud of their contribution during such dark times.

Inevitably, the most acutely high-profile challenge of this period concerned students working towards National 5, Higher and Advanced Higher qualifications. With no way to run the traditional, in-person exams diet, the Scottish Government ordered a switch to teacher-generated grades and tasked the Scottish Qualifications Authority (SQA) with developing a fair and workable system for certifying pupils.

What happened next was, without doubt, the biggest education scandal of Scotland's devolution era, and did enormous damage to many people's faith in both the system itself and those running it. The emergency protocol developed by the SQA required teachers across the country to use whatever material students had already generated, combined with their professional judgements on any likely development in the final months of the course, to determine an appropriate grade for each person in their class. So far, so sensible. The grade would be an 'estimate' in that it would be predictive, but it would also be based on an analysis of all the student's work over the course of the year. As a result, this approach could in fact be more accurate than an exam score, depending on what it is that you are actually trying to measure.

Teachers had been working with their students for most of the year by the time schools closed, and when you factor in the Easter holidays, exam prep and study leave, the amount of actual lost teaching time was limited. They also have plenty of experience reaching assessment judgements, given that doing this on a daily basis is, fundamentally, what the process of teaching is all about. Of course, it would be better not to switch to an entirely teacher-led system overnight and under such difficult circumstances, and there can be issues with teachers overestimating their own students' likely exam performance, but trusting the profession was always the best way forward. In fact, it was always the only way forward.

The SQA and Scottish Government disagreed. Neither had

any intention of trusting teachers, respecting their professional judgements or – worst of all – prioritising the needs and wellbeing of young people. Instead, they did what many feared – they set about protecting the system, even if that had to be done at the expense of pupils.

In a normal year, pupils' results are technically broken down into bands, and we have an upper and lower band for each passing grade from A – C: a band 1 is an upper A, for example, while a band 4 is a lower B. This largely invisible process has no real impact for students, and is ultimately a statistical exercise. With exams cancelled, the easiest thing to do would have been to simply ask teachers to assign each student an A, B, C or Fail grade, completely freeing them to make the fairest overall decision for every young person; instead, the SQA decided not only to maintain the banding system but to expand upon it. Rather than reducing bureaucracy, they strengthened their grip on the final profile of the results by breaking down the grades to a total of 19 sub-bands, some of which represented just a 2% window.

The entire system was obviously ludicrous to anyone with even the slightest understanding of the situation teachers and pupils faced. It wasn't enough to know that a student, based on all the work they had done and the trajectory on which they had been travelling, deserved a B – teachers had to decide whether they should receive an upper or lower B, and then decide whether to award an upper or lower upper or lower B. If a student was a lower A, their teacher had to place them as an upper lower A, a middle lower A, or a lower lower A. There were six different options available that all meant a pupil had failed. The whole thing was an extravagant display of bureaucratic idiocy which, even in these early stages, clearly stemmed from a refusal to trust teachers and a desire to protect the system rather than students.

Incredibly, there was worse to come. Once the class-level

grade sub-bands had been decided, all of that information had to be pulled together at school level, with pupils then ranked within each sub-band. In a big enough school, that would mean dividing pupil performance down to fractions of percentage points, which is obviously ridiculous. Teachers had already assigned their students the grades they deserved, so why on earth were they now, in the middle of a pandemic, being forced to play one student off against another and rank them in a perverse internal school league table? There was one simple, and inevitably disastrous, reason: to allow the SQA statisticians to overrule teachers in order to keep their data in line and their graphs stable.

If the SQA looked at the information submitted by a school and found, for example, that more As had been awarded than they deemed appropriate, they would simply start unilaterally changing pupils' grades based on the ranking system. Those ranked near the bottom of the lowest sub-groups in each grade band would therefore be at risk of having their A reduced to a B, a B turned in to a C, or even a pass switched to a fail. But how could the SQA decide what an appropriate set of grades would look like for each school? The answer was that they would use past results data to establish an acceptable range and then make changes to keep grades aligned to these historic trends. And thus, the now infamous 'algorithm' was born.

We already knew of the near-iron link between affluence and outcomes, and that schools in wealthy areas get better exam results than those serving deprived communities simply because they are located in wealthy areas. What the SQA and Scottish Government did was set out to make sure things stayed that way, because if the results strayed too much, and if too many poor kids were allowed to do too well, then the 'credibility' of the system (and, coincidentally of course, the advantages enjoyed by the middle classes) might be at risk. It was, and will always remain, an utterly unforgivable decision, one that would see brilliant kids in poor areas penalised while average pupils in rich areas were protected.

This was as clear an example of class-based discrimination as you will find – and it was all absolutely intentional.

When the results were released at the beginning of August, both the SQA and the SNP government insisted that the system had worked well. In their news release, the government highlighted that pass rates for National 5, Higher and Advanced Higher had all slightly increased, and also suggested that, without the SQA intervention, the increases would have been simply too high to be 'credible'. They even shamelessly tried to herald 'a narrowing of the attainment gap at grades A–C between the most and least disadvantaged young people'. But this was merely an act of political sleight of hand to hide the truth. In reality, nearly 125,000 results had been reduced and their attempts to 'correct' the system had – as predicted – had a far bigger impact on the poorest kids than on the richest: the algorithm reduced the Highers pass rate for those from the most deprived parts of Scotland by 15.2 percentage points, more than twice the rate experienced by the wealthiest pupils. With too many young people doing too well, those running the system targeted those with least when trying to level things back out.

It's worth taking a moment to explore that increase in pass rates, which has been much commented upon but scarcely explained, and which many interpreted as 'grade inflation' by teachers. In a normal year with a regular exam diet, it is the exam itself that divides students into their final grades – and those grades aren't necessarily any sort of reflection of the student's knowledge, skills, abilities, consistency or development over the year. It doesn't really matter how our young people have performed throughout their course (an obvious, inescapable and crippling flaw in the system that desperately needs to be addressed) because it is the final exams, plus some coursework marks in certain subjects, that determine results. What's more, pass marks and grade boundaries are adjusted each year to keep the stats in line. If too many people are going to pass, then the bar is adjusted to make sure that the required number of (mostly poorer) people fail.

Imagine you have ten students who, throughout the year, have been right on the borderline between a pass and a fail, always meeting the minimum standards required of the course, but never significantly exceeding them. In a system using examinations, half of that group might fail each year – because the system is predicated on the assumption that a certain number of pupils *must* fail – but there is no way to know in advance which half it will be. Every year teachers send such pupils in to sit exams hoping that they have a good day, get a good paper, and manage to pass, but knowing that some of them won't. If we're really honest, it's a bit of a lottery.

Without those exams, there is no way to determine which pupils from the borderline group should be issued a failing grade and which ones should pass. With no system in place to determine which individuals should be sacrificed to the bell curve, the only logical, professional and ethical response is to err on the side of the kids coping with a deadly pandemic and award a pass to all of the borderline pupils who have met the required standard during the year.

Think about it this way: in normal years we ignored students' actual abilities and concentrated almost entirely on their performance on a single day, grinding them through an assessment system set up to fail a guaranteed number of pupils each year and calling it a meritocracy – but when those rigged exams were removed, and the means by which we supress results temporarily abandoned, pass rates and A grades increased.

This wasn't grade inflation – it was grade correction. And it should have raised serious questions about the treatment of young people in all those allegedly normal years: just how many students have had their lives altered, their hopes curtailed, by a system focused more on statistical consistency than fairness and accuracy?

Depressingly, though unsurprisingly, neither the government nor the SQA had any intention of entering into such a discussion. The priority was protecting the system and if that meant individual pupils paying the price then so be it. The results would stand. The message to thousands of young people was clear and horrifying: your postcode defines you. Know your place.

Fortunately, there were plenty who disagreed, not least the young people who had been treated with such appalling disregard. Some of them began to protest, refusing to tolerate the discrimination to which they were being subjected, and gathering significant media coverage in the process. More and more stories began to emerge of young people who had worked hard and been predicted high grades only to have them pulled down for no other reason than where they lived. With each passing day the injustice being more stark and the pressure built. The SNP desperately tried to keep a grip of the situation, but it quickly became clear that this was not a controversy that would simply blow over or that could be triangulated away. Kids' futures were at stake.

Finally, on 11 August, a week after the results had been issued, John Swinney stood up in parliament and said this:

> Presiding Officer, the Covid pandemic has inflicted much suffering and hardship on our society. Many of our young people have had to face that pain across different aspects of their lives.
>
> I want to make clear I understand that anguish and I can see that, for some, the SQA results process made that worse. We set out to ensure that the system was fair. We set out to ensure it was credible. But we did not get it right for all young people.

Before I go any further, I want to apologise for that.

In speaking directly to the young people affected by the downgrading of awards – the 75,000 pupils whose teacher estimates were higher than their final award – I want to say this: I am sorry.

It was an astonishing and humiliating U-turn, fronted by the man who had been made education secretary precisely because of his reputation for unimpeachable competence, and it was followed by a confirmation that every single downgraded result would be restored to the original teacher judgement. The government may have ultimately (and with great reluctance) agreed to do the right thing and abandon the discriminatory algorithm, but by the time they did so thousands and thousands of mostly working-class young people had been forced to endure hellish levels of anxiety as they saw their futures being taken away from them.

The algorithm was not quite dead – the largely well-off students whose grades were increased by it got to hold on to their additional advantage, and we have never really reckoned with the possibility that some grades may have been artificially reduced in anticipation of the SQA moderation system – but at least its worst effects would be largely undone.

The scandal wasn't over, however, because a few weeks later new data emerged which revealed the true scale of what the SQA and government had attempted. Using Freedom of Information laws, I forced the SQA to release data showing the effect of the algorithm on every single high school in Scotland, including specific information on the number of grades reduced from a pass to a fail. Working with education researcher Barry Black, this information was then combined with data showing the proportion of pupils at each state school in receipt of free school meals. In schools where 40% or more of pupils receive free school meals an average of more than 20% of Higher grades were moved from a pass to a fail. In schools with the lowest

Exam Results: Higher Grades Changed from Pass to Fail by SQA Algorithm (Free School Meals) 2020

Source: SQA, Freedom of Information response

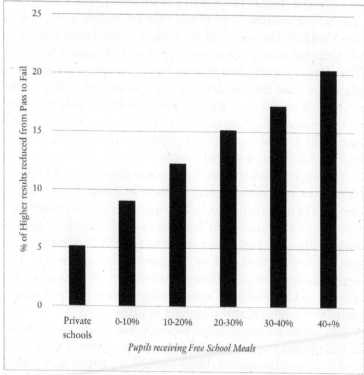

levels of pupils on free school meals the equivalent figure was less than 10%. In private schools it was 5.1%.

The same pattern was found when looking at total downgrades. Schools with the highest numbers of deprived students saw nearly 40% of all grades reduced while those with the lowest numbers of deprived students had slightly more than 20% of grades pulled down by the SQA. Again, private schools came off best.

Using school-level free schools meals data as opposed to

SIMD breakdowns was vital because this is the level at which the SQA algorithm operated. It was, after all, the past performance of a school that influenced whether a pupil would be allowed to keep the grades their teachers awarded, not that pupil's specific circumstances, so it was only by analysing the impact at school level that we could see, with horrifying clarity, the scale of discrimination against working-class kids across Scotland. The story was published by *The Ferret*, an online investigative platform, and the *Sunday National* newspaper, despite the objections of the SQA. We also made all of the data available to the public, allowing anyone to find out what would have happened at their local school if the government and the SQA had not been forced to back down.

You would think that such a massive scandal would at least have led to some consequences for those in charge. You would be wrong. The head of the SQA (who happens to have formerly been Director of Learning at the Scottish Government) kept her job and her absurdly high salary despite overseeing an indefensible grading system that had to be completely abandoned. The organisation's clearly ill-equipped board of management, which is made up of 27% management consultants and zero% classroom teachers, also remained in place.

Education secretary John Swinney had to go through the ordeal of sitting solemnly while a few of his political opponents said some mildly unkind things about him, before surviving a vote of no confidence with the help of Scottish Green Party MSPs. Nicola Sturgeon, who at one time had wanted to be judged on her record, and who had also defended the discriminatory algorithm, managed to avoid scrutiny almost entirely. Consequences and accountability are, it seems, reserved for little people.

But the question remains: how did things go so badly wrong in the first place? Are we really to believe that the people in charge of the system couldn't see what everyone else could? Is it actually credible to accept that ministers, advisers and officials didn't understand the entirely inevitable consequences of their decisions?

The far more likely explanation is that they understood the consequences of their socioeconomic algorithm perfectly well, and could foresee its effects just like the rest of us. They knew that a system based on schools' past results would disadvantage pupils in deprived areas, and they recognised that young people would have their grades lowered for no other reason than where they had grown up. They knew all of this because the system had been created to ensure that historic patterns, with all the class-based inequalities underlying them, were repeated in 2020. That was precisely the point. It was a feature, not a bug, and it was the mechanism by which the government and SQA attempted to balance the educational books on the backs of the poor.

Ask yourself this: if the algorithm had threatened to demonstrably disadvantage the children of middle-class families, if ground zero was going to be East Renfrewshire rather than Easterhouse, do you think there is any chance whatsoever that it would have been implemented and defended by the government and SQA? I don't believe so, and I don't expect that many of you do either.

A Disrupted School Year

In May 2020, the Scottish Government announced that schools would reopen in the coming August using a 'blended' model of learning. This would see pupils spend some of their time in school and the rest at home learning remotely.

There was no single national approach or standard – other than trying to maximise the time pupils could spend with their teachers – for the simple reason that it would have been impossible. Every school in the country had to figure out how many pupils could be in their building at a given time, how to arrange appropriate transport to get them there, and even how to maximise the availability of teachers (many of whom, let's not forget, had their own children at home requiring care and attention). Scotland's 2500 schools come in all shapes and sizes, and serve communities ranging from tightly packed inner-city streets to sparsely populated islands. A one-size-fits-all approach would only have done more harm, and the government was right to resist pressure to attempt to impose one.

With just weeks to go until the start of the summer break, schools raced to design rotas that would enable the delivery of the blended model to the best of their abilities. Unfortunately, the wide (and inevitable) variations in provision across the country which became quickly apparent stoked continuing controversy. Particular anxieties were expressed over the different degrees to which live, online lessons were being offered to pupils, despite the fact that this is about the least effective way to manage a system of online learning. There was, and remains, a strong feeling that many of those complaining about this apparently unacceptable failure were more interested in securing a remote babysitter for themselves than an effective education for their kids.

Critics (including Baron McConnell of Glenscorrodale) argued that the Scottish Government or local councils should effectively requisition buildings to ensure that every child could be accommodated full-time as normal, but those same people never seemed willing or able to grapple with the practicalities of their demands when it came to issues such as resources, timetabling, transport, security, staffing or safeguarding. Then, on 23 of June, in the face of huge pressure and with Covid restrictions easing as case numbers fell, the government announced that schools would in fact reopen fully in August. This would prove to be a critical mistake, robbing schools and families of the chance to test out their blended learning plans in relatively controlled circumstances, and storing up that rapid learning curve for when the actual emergency arrived – as it always would – a few months later.

Over the weeks and months that followed the summer, a steady trickle of Covid disruption turned rapidly into a flood. More and more pupils and teachers were forced into self-isolation, either through positive tests or identification as a close contact of another infected person, with every single absence having knock-on effects that multiplied the problems over and over. Many teachers complained about their treatment during this period: Glasgow's Director of Education was forced to apologise after sending a memo to staff that seemed to blame them for increasing Covid cases in schools, and in Aberdeen teachers were told to switch off the NHS Track and Trace app while at work. By the start of December all National 5, Higher and Advanced Higher exams had been cancelled – at least in theory.

And then came the hammer blow: on the 4th of January 2021 the Scottish Government announced another lockdown as part of a desperate effort to control the rapid spread of coronavirus cases and subsequent spike in deaths. Schools would not reopen as planned after the Christmas and New Year holiday, and pupils would have to learn remotely.

Once again schools had been given no time to put plans in place. This is because government was desperate to keep schools open, which is of course understandable, but the feeling was that it ultimately became political, and that meant that decisions that should have been taken early (in order to benefit pupils, parents and teachers) were delayed until the last minute (in order to benefit politicians).

Nor were teachers able, as some thought, to just turn to the plans that had been made before the summer but never used. Those had been designed for a blended model, not fully remote delivery, and for pupils who were at the start of the school year rather than halfway through it. This meant that an incredible amount of material had to be created almost overnight, and technical problems that should had been dealt with the previous

August became a serious barrier.

To make matters worse, an FOI response in March 2021 showed that the government had failed to meet its target for distributing 70,000 laptops and tablets to pupils in need. A goal of providing 18,000 internet connections was also missed, and apparently wide variations in access across the country fuelled existing concerns about the impact of the school closures on the poorest pupils. In some homes, pupils had their own devices, space to work and support when they needed it; in others, families were sharing a single tablet and an unreliable broadband connection in a confined and claustrophobic space.

Schools reopened to the youngest pupils first, as they were regarded as being the least able to learn online as well as being unlikely to contract or spread the virus, but all pupils did not return to their classrooms until after the Easter holidays.

2021 Results Shambles

Even by the time the new school year started in August 2020, it had been clear for months that the exams planned for the following May would not go ahead. Everyone could see that the chances of the country getting through the autumn and winter without massive pandemic-related disruption were effectively zero, meaning that even if circumstances did allow mass indoor gatherings by exam time, a national exam diet taking no account of individual and local circumstances couldn't possibly be fair to pupils.

Clearly rattled and lacking confidence after the catastrophe of the 2020 results scandal, a much-diminished John Swinney seemed unable to make tough calls at the right time, and schools started the academic year without any certainty as to how it would end for students in National 5, Higher and Advanced Higher courses. At an organisational level that was a shocking failure, and the problems were then compounded by several months of dither, delay and cowardly indecision.

There was no way the government could possibly even come close to guaranteeing that a regular exam diet would take place in 2021, and that being the case there was only ever one sensible and responsible course of action: to announce its cancellation as early as possible. Had this been done before the summer then plans could have been in place for a consistent but light-touch framework outlining how teachers should determine grades in 2021, with variation between subjects as necessary and room built-in to allow for the disruption caused by pupil and teacher absences and even, if it came to it, nationwide school closures.

Unfortunately, we got pretty much exactly the opposite. Those in charge clung to the delusion that normal exams under normal conditions would go ahead, even in the most abnormal times that anyone had ever seen. It was as if the government was hoping that the pandemic would just magically melt away and everything would be alright, but in failing to confront reality – whether that was driven by politics or incompetence – they failed young people all over again. Even when the cancellation of exams did come, they couldn't bring themselves to just get on with it. National 5 exams were cancelled in October but, at this stage, Higher and Advanced Higher exams were still supposed to be going ahead, with a two-week delay to their starting date apparently making all the difference. It was obvious to pretty much everyone working in education that this was nonsense, but teachers were nonetheless left in yet another impossible position: they had to keep working as if those exams would be taking place, even though they knew it wasn't going to happen. As such, even more time was wasted and the pressure on teachers and their pupils just continued to increase.

By the time the government finally worked up the courage to do the right thing and cancel all 2021 school exams, which happened at the beginning of December 2020, it was far too late. Schools were just a few weeks away from the Christmas and New Year holidays, around halfway through their academic year, and would of course have to cope with a near zero notice, panicked switch to remote learning from January 2021. And then, to make things worse, the SQA had to get involved. The exams body – still led by the people who had failed so comprehensively the year before – was charged with developing another alternative certification system which once again, but for different reasons, descended into farce.

There would be no algorithm this year, and no arrogant alteration of pupils' grades once they had been submitted, but simply trusting the teaching profession clearly wasn't an option either. Right from the start it felt an awful lot like the SQA was still in a huff over all the entirely justified criticism it had already received. Having apparently had no proper contingency plans in place at the start of the school year, guidance gradually emerged explaining how teachers should arrive at their decisions over what grades to award, with an emphasis on 'demonstrated attainment' and exams that were as close to 'normal' as possible. This model was designed to cope with the cancellation of National 5 exams only, and to work in a system where education was being disrupted but, crucially, schools remained open. It might even have been just about workable (although still unfair) under those circumstances, but it was never going to be able to cope with full-scale exam cancellation *and* the school closures that took place at the start of 2021.

The biggest difference between the 2020 system and that put in place the following year was the type of evidence that would be permitted when determining students' results. In 2020, teachers had been able to assign grades based on 'inferred attainment', which meant that they could use their professional judgement to take a student's circumstances into account: they didn't necessarily need a piece of paper with an A grade on it in order to award an A to someone who clearly deserved it. This time – despite the false claims of various people up to and including the First Minister – teachers would not be able to genuinely apply their professional judgement to decide grades; instead, it would be all about having those pieces of paper, with that reality partially obscured behind the euphemism of 'demonstrated attainment.' For whatever reason, both the SQA and government actually seemed set on erecting, rather than demolishing, barriers to young people's progress.

The specifics of the guidance around demonstrating students' attainment levels varied from subject to subject. In some there seemed to be wiggle room in the final assessment approach but in others things were tightly controlled. In National 5 physics, for example, the SQA listed the following as 'the key pieces of evidence' that would be required for students:

- An examination, covering as much of the course as possible
- A second, top-up examination or an extended test, that includes those areas not assessed in the first examination
- End-of-topic tests, including grade A marks, which you may use as supplementary evidence only, as they are not as reliable for estimating grades.

As a result, although the national level exam diet had been cancelled, young people across the country simply found themselves sitting a school-level exam diet that in many cases was more onerous than what they would have faced in a normal year. Although it was theoretically possible to meet the SQA's demands without adopting this approach, in practice the only manageable way for most schools to generate results within the new rules was to either directly replicate an end-of-year exam timetable or, in an attempt to make things more manageable for pupils, break up these final tests into a number of sittings. The latter approach meant that young people would be spared two-and-three-hour exams, but in exchange many found themselves facing all but continuous assessments for weeks, or pass marks that were increased to reflect the eased assessment conditions. All of this, remember, came after months of disrupted education following by an extended period of remote learning.

Official question papers were provided by the SQA and it soon became clear that teaching staff would be expected to both mark their students' exams-that-weren't-exams and also moderate the marking of other schools in their area. The sheer scale of the workload imposed on the profession was extraordinary, and although the Scottish Government reluctantly decided to offer a £400 (before tax) payment for this work, their own officials noted that for many this would end up being less than the minimum wage. On top of that, part-time members of staff would be paid less, even if they were doing just as much or even more work than some of their full-time colleagues, and support staff would be excluded from the payments no matter how much work they had done to help ensure that results could be submitted for pupils.

All the while, both the government and the SQA insisted that exams really had been cancelled and that teacher judgement was at the heart of the system. It was nonsense, and even as young people – energised by their successful fight against the injustices of 2020 – began to speak out in the press, accusing the SQA of imposing exams by stealth and highlighting the impact on their wellbeing and mental health, those in charge refused to listen. Having been forced into a U-turn the year before, the powers that be clearly had no intention of allowing it to happen again.

Almost as soon as schools began to run their exam diets, details of the SQA papers – and in some cases images of the papers themselves – began to appear on social media. Students also used anonymous Discord servers to share extensive information about the exams, and it was by this point clear that significant numbers would now be sitting tests that they had already seen in advance: in a members' survey by the Scottish Secondary Teachers Association (SSTA), around two thirds of respondents said that their students had sat the SQA paper unaltered. It was an entirely inevitable turn of events, yet it somehow seemed to take the SQA by surprise. In May they issued a letter threatening the young people involved in a pointless but sadly predictable attempt to shift the blame for their own failures. Concerns were also raised about the different levels of support and opportunity that seemed to be available to pupils from one school to another. For example, while some young people were given only one attempt to 'demonstrate their attainment' others had the chance to be reassessed if their teachers felt that they had underperformed. This was technically within the rules, but it seems likely to have benefited young people whose schools serve more affluent areas and, in particular, those in private education.

By the end of May the credibility of the system had begun to collapse. The model of 'demonstrated attainment' was shown to be a demonstrably unfair approach, one that once again sought to protect the system rather than pupils. Despite the government's insistence that, unlike in 2020, past results would not be used to change a student's grades, it emerged that every council in the country had in fact used historic results data as part of their moderation process for 2021. So while it was true that the SQA would not be applying any algorithm to results *once they had been submitted*, pressure was applied at the other end of the process in an attempt to push grades back towards past trends in each school. The practicalities may have changed but the underlying principle that had driven the 2020 scandal – that even during a pandemic the stability and predictability of the data was more important than the wellbeing of young people – was alive and well.

In response to several Freedom of Information requests, the Scottish Government and local councils provided details of the ways in which past data was being used as part of the results process. In Dundee, for example, schools were issued with a 'Toolkit taking into account attainment data over the last five years against working grades and provisional results'; in Angus, schools would be 'sense checking' their grades 'using data from the three years prior to 2020'; where schools in Renfrewshire identified 'variances' from past results patterns, they were expected to 'request moderation support from the local authority to ensure National Standards have been applied'; in Fife, schools were 'provided with a spreadsheet of subject data at each level' in order to 'allow consideration of statistical significance' when assigning grades. Where results differed from historical trends, many councils would demand that school staff provide 'context' or a 'rationale'. Nice set of results you've got there, they seemed to say, but wouldn't it be a shame if something happened to it?

So, while teachers' assessment decisions may not have been directly (or, to use the government's preferred term, unilaterally) changed by the SQA, schools were put under broad pressure to keep results within expectations that, as with the 2020 algorithm, had been determined by the past performance – and therefore the relative affluence – of each school. What's more, the results from 2020 were not included in the comparison data, meaning that those pupils receiving their grades in 2021, when schooling was even more disrupted than it had been in the previous year, were being measured against pre-pandemic benchmarks: information from the only other vaguely comparable year, when results just so happen to have gone up, was deliberately and explicitly excluded.

As usual, concerns over the reliability, transparency and basic fairness of the system were waved away by those in power who insisted – just as they had the year before – that all of the teachers, parents, pupils and academics criticising their plans were wrong. Incredibly, even the country's biggest teaching union, the Educational Institute of Scotland (EIS), stepped in to protect the government and SQA, although this may have had something to do with the fact that its leaders had been part of the group that approved the new framework in the first place. Even a claimed 'investigation' into the process, mentioned briefly by new education secretary Shirley-Anne Somerville, turned out to be little more than a cynical manipulation of the situation, with an FOI release revealing that officials had simply emailed each council and asked a pair of carefully phrased yes/no questions designed to provide exactly the information that the government was seeking.

I am writing the final paragraphs of this chapter on the day when the 2021 results have been released. Although individual pupils already knew what grades they would receive, the national level data, including some information about the impact of the system on pupils from deprived backgrounds, is now available.

Higher pass rates have dropped, which is hardly a surprise given that the SQA and Scottish Government set out to suppress them, and you will, I'm sure, be shocked to discover that the decline for pupils from the poorest areas was more than double that recorded by those from the richest parts of the country. The percentage of A grades overall has gone up but, once again, pupils from the wealthiest parts of Scotland have been the main beneficiaries. Other factors have also had an impact: the Highers pass rate for disabled pupils dropped by 5.1 percentage points, but amongst non-disabled pupils the drop was just 2.4 percentage points.

So far, however, the data that has been released is extremely limited and, like last year, FOI requests will clearly be needed in order to reveal the full picture. For example, we need to analyse the pass rates of different subjects and of individual schools, (including private schools) to understand the full effects of the 2021 approach. More detailed deprivation breakdowns will also be needed because the SQA has, for whatever reason, only divided pupils up into five SIMD groups, not the full ten that are available.

But for now the situation is largely as expected: after a second year of massive disruption to schools, and having been placed in the firing line last year before the now famous U-turn, the system has once again ensured that lose with least are placed at the greatest disadvantage.

7

Finding Out What Works

DESPITE ALL THE obvious issues in Scotland's schools, a selection of which have been explored over the previous chapters, there is still nothing whatsoever to be gained from assuming all is lost or, conversely, trying to endlessly reinvent the same wheels. There's a place for new ideas, but a massive range of great ideas already exist. If we look across our own country, and across the world, we can find all sorts of policies, ideas and initiatives that could improve the experiences of young people in our schools.

While doing so, however, we need to keep in mind that context is crucial. No matter how badly we want to make things better, an education system, like any other, can only cope with so much change at once, and things are even more difficult when everything and everyone is already operating under enormous pressure.

We also do not have the luxury of simply burning the whole thing down and starting again from scratch (even if we wanted to) given the damage that this would do to an entire generation of children caught up in the chaos.

Yet another variable is the impact of different cultures and circumstances between and within countries (including our own) which means that even the best ideas are not automatically transferable: something that is completely normal in southeast Asia might not be possible in Scotland, and an approach that works on Tiree might be a disaster in Cumbernauld.

Celebrating Our Own Success

It is absolutely vital that we have the courage to be honest about the mistakes that have been made and where our current approaches fall short, but it is equally important to recognise the great work being done in schools in every single corner of Scotland – in fact, there's so much of it that it could easily fill a book on its own. The trouble is that, for teachers, being brilliant is just part of the job, and they can be reluctant to shout about their successes.

For all the criticism it faces – much of it driven by political expediency on the one hand and sheer, bloody-minded ignorance on the other – our education system is still one of the best in the world, and the young people who are going through it (including my own son) are still being given a great start in life. We need to celebrate that, so here is a tiny selection of snapshots of the minor miracles that happen all the time in Scotland's schools.

Anti-Poverty Action in Glasgow

Since 2019, four schools in Glasgow – which has some of the worst deprivation rates in all of Scotland – have operated an anti-poverty pilot scheme aimed at supporting families struggling with the complexities of the benefits system.

A financial inclusion officer worked with families at Bellahouston Academy, St Mungo's Academy, Rosshall Academy and St Paul's High School, directing them towards welfare payments to which they were entitled but, through a lack of knowledge, had thus far not accessed. These include free school meals, educational maintenance allowance, young carer grants and state benefits.

In a little more than a year, families across the four pilot schools claimed an additional £700,000, and the scheme has been so successful that it will now be rolled out to all secondary schools in the city. Rather than concentrating of addressing the symptoms of poverty, this project has focused on reducing the poverty itself.

STEM in South-West Scotland

In 2019, as part of efforts to improve and enhance the education on offer at schools throughout the area, Dumfries and Galloway council identified ten 'key sectors for economic growth' across the region. Seven of these include components that are directly relevant to education in science, technology, engineering and maths (STEM). To help ensure that school leavers have the skills and knowledge they need in these areas, it was decided to focus on developing STEM teaching not just in secondary schools but also for primary pupils.

One of the ways in which this is being pursed is through the use of The Bridge, an educational facility in Dumfries intended to 'help learners develop specialist skills and knowledge that they need for further education and work'. The four secondary schools in the town have aligned their timetables to take advantage of the range of courses on offer, but the facilities have also been used to give primary school pupils, and their teachers, access to resources and learning experiences that would otherwise be unavailable. Lessons at The Bridge have been built around themes including Food & Drink, Energy Sources & Sustainability, and Visual Programming and Genetics.

QR Codes to Boost Wellbeing

In order to encourage pupils to seek support when they need it, Springfield Primary School in West Lothian has used modern technology to set up an easy-to-use way of doing so.

Each pupil has a 'trusted adult' whom they can approach for help. If they would like to talk to them, the pupil can visit a display in the school corridor showing a picture of each adult alongside a QR code. By scanning this code with a mobile device, the pupil is automatically taken to a short online form where they can enter their name and how urgently they need support. A notification is sent to the relevant adult who can then arrange a meeting with the pupil.

Systems like this enable young people to get the help they require quickly and confidentially, encouraging them to be more honest about their own needs and more confident in accessing support.

Legal Studies for School Pupils

As a result of a partnership between the school and the University of Glasgow, formed thanks to a history teacher who originally studied law, students at Clydebank High School – which serves one of the more deprived catchments in Scotland – are now able to participate in a Legal Studies course as part of timetabled classes in sixth year. The course isn't a Higher but rather a National Progression Award, so still counts as a level 6 qualification. Although there are no formal admissions criteria, students would generally be expected to have already passed Highers in English and at least one social subject such as History or Modern Studies.

Students study two mandatory units, Introduction to Scots Law and Crime & Society, but what really makes the course stand out is that it has no final exam. Instead, students are assessed on an ongoing basis throughout the year. This not only removes some of the overall pressures for those taking part but it also allows the class teacher to concentrate on educating, rather than coaching, their students. Even in its first year the course saw success with several young people applying, and being accepted, to study law at university.

Positive Destinations Against the Odds

Lochend Community High School in Glasgow's east end serves one of the most deprived areas in the whole of Scotland: more than 90% of pupils come from the poorest fifth of postcode areas in the country, and it is the only school where more than half of pupils receive free school meals.

Despite all this, Lochend has also become the first school in Glasgow to see every single one of its leavers go on to a positive destination.

This extraordinary feat has been achieved at least in part through the effective use of Pupil Equity Funding, which has been used to pay the salary of a dedicated employability officer focused on ensuring that those leaving school have the best possible opportunities. The school also provides support to former pupils for up to six months after they leave and has formed strong links with local organisations and businesses.

In 2020, 21% of Lochend school leavers went to higher education, a further 62% moved on to further education, 8% joined training schemes and 9% found work (with none of that final group employed on zero-hours contracts). In the coming years those involved are hopeful that more pupils will begin applying to university courses, although the central goal is simply to do the very best for every single young person as they take their first steps after school.

Community and Diversity

In May 2016, a little primary school in the southside of Glasgow attracted the attention of the *Daily Mail*, who described it using the following headline: 'The Glasgow primary without a *single* Scottish pupil: 181 of school's 222 children are from either Romania or Slovakia'.

Annette Street is located in Govanhill, one of the city's most diverse neighbourhoods and a regular target for racists seeking to sow and exploit division. The article in question, sparked by a crowdfunder set up to help the school buy new games and materials, immediately set out to ring the alarm bells over the school's 'mainly Eastern European children', drawing particular attention to the fact that 'four out of five young students are from the families of Roma immigrants'.

The following week, however, the school was featured in a *Daily Record* article that celebrated, rather than lamented, the cultural and linguistic diversity of the children and their families, as well as their connections to Scotland. It highlighted the multilingual skills of pupils, their area's history of welcoming immigrants, and perhaps most pertinently, a banner declaring: 'One Scotland Many Cultures'.

In 2018, Annette Street Primary School was declared a national winner of the First Minister's Reading Challenge.

Outdoors in Inveraray

At Inveraray Primary School, outdoor learning is an absolutely central feature. Like many schools, pupils enjoy a mixture of formal and informal outdoor learning experiences, from putting their maths and literacy knowledge into action to engaging in child-led, exploratory play.

What makes this school stand out is the commitment to this aspect of learning. Rather than squeezing in the odd session here or there, teachers have decided to assign dedicated time for being outside: for the oldest pupils, this means a quarter of their time is spent outdoors while for the youngest this rises to a full 50%. A forest school in a nearby estate and a beach school on the shores of the Loch Fyne provide a wealth of invaluable experiences, helping to develop young people's confidence, resilience and collaborative abilities.

Despite the pressures of post-lockdown learning in March 2021, the school stuck to its philosophy, retaining the focus on outdoor learning when it would have been easy to play it safe, keeps the kids in class, and adopt a more traditional approach. The result? Literacy and numeracy levels that not only exceeded those pre-Covid, but were also higher than 2019 national averages.

The Happiness Squad

At Victoria Primary school in Edinburgh, one primary 3 class has set up the 'Happiness Squad', a team of young people who praise and celebrate their classmates at the end of each day.

The squad is rotated on a daily basis, with five or six members each time, and lines up at the school gate with banners and big smiles to cheer for their friends as they head home.

Having begun on little more than a whim, the experience has been so positive that the school is now looking to expand the idea to incorporate other classes, as well as find opportunities to allow young people to complement the activities with their own creative abilities like music and dance.

Syrian Success in the Highlands and Islands

In recent years several thousand Syrian refugees have been welcomed to Scotland after fleeing the conflict in their homeland. Although there is sometimes a presumption that refugees and asylum seekers are accommodated only in urban areas, Syrian families have been accepted by communities across the country including, of course, those in the Highlands and Islands.

At Thurso High School, children from Syrian families have benefitted from an expanded curriculum and have already achieved a range of qualifications including English for Speakers of Other Languages (ESOL), business, administration and maths.

Meanwhile, at Stornoway Primary School on Lewis, primary six pupil Abdullah Al Nakeeb has made headlines after winning a national award for progress in Gaelic; his younger brother Majd had been recognised for his own achievements in learning the language a few months earlier.

Celtic Youth Academy

Since 2009, Celtic Football Club has operated a partnership with St Ninian's High School in Kirkintilloch. The programme allows boys on the books at Celtic to transfer to the school from outwith the area, meaning that they can complete their secondary education as part of the scheme. Those involved train at lunchtime and after school and follow a more flexible timetable allowing further football sessions instead of certain classes. At the end of the day, some are transported to the nearby Celtic training ground at Lennoxtown (where they have their evening meal and complete further sessions) while others complete their training using the school facilities before going home. Those who live too far away to travel can also be supported with local accommodation during the week.

The partnership means that those involved can combine their football development with academic progress, thereby increasing their chances of progressing to first team football while helping to ensure an appropriate educational safety net for those who do not make it as professionals. Nearly 200 boys have already progressed through the scheme, the most famous of whom is Scotland international Kieran Tierney.

Time for Inclusive Education

Although not necessarily a school-level development, or one led by education professionals, it would be absurd to discuss success stories in Scottish education without recognising the enormous impact of Time for Inclusive Education (TIE).

Founded in 2015 by Jordan Daly and Liam Stevenson, the

campaign sought to ensure that all schools provide an educational experience that is LGBTQ+ inclusive as part of efforts to tackle homophobic, biphobic and transphobic bullying. A major part of their approach has been to fight for LGBTQ+ visibility in schools, including within the curriculum, by running powerful workshops and highlighting a wide range of LGBTQ+ role models whose achievements can be explored in the classroom.

In 2017 a majority of Scottish parliamentarians supported the TIE campaign; the following year, the Scottish Government accepted more than 30 recommendations and pledged to make LGBTQ+ inclusive education a reality in every state school across the country. There is no doubt whatsoever that the work of TIE has changed, and almost certainly saved, lives throughout Scotland, and while we rightly ask what we can learn from other countries, this is an area where perhaps we can be the inspiration for others.

How Others See Us

Recognising our successes, and sharing them with others, is an important piece in the puzzle of improving Scottish education, but it can also be useful to gather outside opinions and, to borrow that famous line, see ourselves as others see us. In Scotland, those outside perspectives have come from two main sources: the Organisation for Economic Cooperative and Development (OECD) and the Scottish Government's International Council of Education Advisers (ICEA).

ICEA Reports

In 2016, the Scottish Government established an 'International Council of Education Advisers'. It brought together members from a range of countries in order to 'advise ministers on how best to achieve excellence and equity' in the Scottish education system. The council members are well-regarded experts from countries including Finland, Singapore, and Canada, although the original membership, for reasons known only to the SNP, also included a banker.

The first formal report of the ICEA was published in June 2018. It recognised a number of 'key strengths' in Scottish education, including the dual focus on excellence and equity, the narrowing attainment gap (albeit based on data which, as we have seen, is questionable at best), and the establishment of regional bodies to support collaboration between schools and councils (known as Regional Improvement Collaboratives, or RICs). It even described CfE as 'forward-looking' and 'the cornerstone of educational transformation in Scotland.'

The report also included 19 supposedly 'specific' recommendations such as:

- Consider how the current policies aimed at improving the education system, and those in the future, support the full aspirations of CfE so that young people in Scotland can continue to fulfil their potential.
- Consider how improvement in the health and wellbeing of young people is defined, gauged and evaluated so any progress can be clearly established and validated with any negative effects avoided.
- Replace the terminology of reform with the language of improvement. Set out an explicit theory of change that underpins and supports the current strategies and approaches to educational improvement, which will help to identify the conditions that need to be in place for the aims of the educational improvement programme to be achieved.

There are, in fairness, specific recommendations in there – the second item in the list, for example, basically means: you need better data about stuff that isn't exam results – but much of it is buried in the sort of language that makes it very difficult for non-specialists to understand, which in turn makes it near impossible to hold government to account on whether or not it acts on the advice it receives. This is not intended as a criticism of the ICEA members – pretty much all official reports use the same sort of language, and just because the published report is extremely diplomatic doesn't mean that face-to-face conversations were not much more direct. Nonetheless, the fact remains that these sorts of materials are of extremely limited practical use if they are not directly accessible to the public, because otherwise the government always has the advantage when it comes to managing expectations and controlling the narrative.

In December 2020, the council released its second formal report, this time focusing on how Scotland can reform its education system in response to the coronavirus pandemic. The council points out that, despite the impact of Covid, 'many education systems in the world are also exploring how they could capitalise on the opportunity to make fundamental changes to their school system'. It once again makes a series of recommendations, this time organised under one of two headings – 'Navigating the Pandemic and Beyond: Redesigning Schooling, Teaching and Learning' and 'Governing and Leading Education System Change and Improvement'.

As with the first report, the recommendations themselves (12 of them this time) are couched in thoroughly technical language: one insists on the need for an 'asset-based view of students' while another encourages government to commit to 'system change that is driven by collaborative professional relationships and underpinned by peer challenge rather than external demands'. If you know how to read it, the document in fact advocates the sort of revolutionary generational shift in schooling that could be legitimately transformative.

This goal is probably best summed up by one particularly

striking paragraph near the end of the report, which comes under the heading 'From Abnormal to Extraordinary':

> This is not a time for getting back to normal. It is not even time to develop a modified new normal. It is time to look to the future to redesign Scottish education as a universally designed system for all contingencies and disruptions. This system can and should develop self-directed learners; provide access to digitally based learning as a human right; transform assessment to be continuous, inclusive and responsive; and ensure that all students and teachers are equipped with online and outdoor capabilities that will be pandemic-proof in the future and significantly better in the present. All of this can and should occur within a universally designed system that becomes increasingly inclusive, responsive, agile and collaborative, with changes in government resource allocations that reflect this shift.

When you get beyond the jargon, this is a call for a radical and quite spectacular reimagining of the structures of Scottish education that would demand, among other things, a total rebuild of the existing exam system, and which reflects precisely the sort of thinking that the country desperately needs. Unfortunately, the language in which the report is written, as well as the chaos unfolding when it was published and the lack of specialist capacity in the media, meant that it received limited attention, although echoes of at least some of it can be seen in a few of the manifesto pledges put forward by the SNP prior to winning the 2021 election. The proposals would, however, push the party, the government, and the country's broader educational establishment well beyond their comfort zones, and demand a level of individual and institutional courage that certainly has not been on display over the past five to ten years.

Only time will tell whether the ICEA's exciting vision for Scottish schooling can ever come to fruition under the leadership of those currently charge.

2021 OECD Report

In 2019, the Scottish Government commissioned a new review of CfE from the OECD. It was hoped that this would help us to 'better understand how the curriculum is being designed and implemented in schools and to identify areas for improvement across the country' – put simply, the report would tell us what is going on and how to make things better. These are, of course, things that you might expect a properly functioning and well-managed education system to be able to do for itself, meaning that the very act of calling in the OECD for the job suggests a lack of critical capacity and, therefore, more serious failures from those in charge.

Many people – myself included – were sceptical from the start, because investigations of this sort are largely technocratic affairs that typically hinge on 'desk-based policy analysis' (someone sitting in an office reading the documents that the government sends them) and carefully controlled interactions. They can be all-too-easily stage managed, a point highlighted by the fact that this review would not accept unsolicited submissions from groups or individuals involved in Scottish education. Realistically, such a process was never going to tell ministers anything that they shouldn't already have known – after all, the government has access to all the same materials as the people running the review – and it would almost certainly end up written in such a way that meant it could never really be used to hold the government to account.

Initially the report was to focus on just the senior phase of secondary schools, but opposition parties demanded that it be expanded to take a far broader view of Curriculum for

OECD Report	Plain English
'Significant efforts were made to engage stakeholders throughout CfE's lifecycle, which contributed to wide support for CfE as a direction of travel for Scottish education. However, there is a gap between stakeholders' involvement and their impact on effective enhancements to CfE implementation.'	The people in charge were keen to make it look like they were listening, but they weren't really.
'The structure, learning practices and assessment approaches in the Senior Phase also need adapting to be consistent with CfE's vision, and to allow for the smooth curriculum experience promised from 3 to 18.'	The way we run s4–6 of secondary school is incompatible with the rest of the curriculum and needs major reform.
'Curriculum design and continuous improvement require time and professional investment, which schools can only achieve with ongoing support from the system.'	CfE makes huge demands of teachers who have never been given the support that they need to make it work.
'However, there is an obvious mismatch in the Scottish system between the curriculum-making role of teachers and the comparatively high class contact hours of teachers across the system.'	Teachers in Scotland clearly spend far too much time in front of their classes which makes it hard for them to do their jobs properly.
'But the constant production and recycling of documentation was often described as "overwhelming", and the terminology used too technical and open to interpretation.'	The mountains of repetitive and unclear paperwork produced by those running the system have made things worse.
'For example, efforts to reduce the attainment gap will not be possible solely through schooling and CfE in particular, as other socioeconomic factors influence learner outcomes. It will require broader coalitions with welfare, housing and health policy, for example.'	If you want to close the attainment gap then you need to focus on improving pupils' lives rather than simply concentrating on their time in the classroom.
'Scotland has not decided how or when it will conduct reviews; to date, including this one, reviews have been in response to a controversy rather than planned and proactive, and they have drawn on expertise external to the system.'	Rather than review the system properly, the government keeps having to be dragged kicking and screaming to do the right thing. It is also unwilling to listen to people working within the Scottish system.

Excellence. The original plan had been to publish the review in February 2021, prior to the Holyrood elections that would follow a few months later, but its release was controversially delayed. The government argued (reasonably, it must be said) that the extensions to the remit and the impact of the global pandemic meant that the original date could not be met. When an early summary of the findings was delivered to government some opposition MSPs made a big show of demanding it be made public, but the OECD unsurprisingly refused to allow this as it did not consider the report to be complete. The final version was ultimately released near the end of June, more than six weeks *after* the SNP had overwhelming won yet another election.

The report recognised the strengths and value of Curriculum for Excellence itself, which it described as 'an inspiring and widely supported philosophy of education' which 'allows for effective curricular practices and for the possibility of a truly fulfilling education for learners'; however, it also offered a damning indictment of the government's recent handling of education and of the entire process that surrounded the implementation of CfE. As expected, however, the document (which runs to around 140 extremely dense pages) is written in the sort of technical, jargonistic language that many find impenetrable and which, consequently, provides significant rhetorical cover for politicians.

The table overleaf gives a few examples. There's plenty more where that came from, but you get the idea. Ultimately, the OECD makes four recommendations, all of which make sense because they simply repackage the messages that teachers, pupils, parents and academics have spent years trying to get the government to hear. Like the rest of the report, however, they too are couched in disappointingly opaque language that will undoubtedly present a barrier for many people and, at the same time, make it easy for the government to claim that it is indeed following the recommendations, whether or not that is in fact the case.

The headline recommendations are:

1 Balance Curriculum for Excellence so students can fully benefit from a coherent learning experience from ages 3 to 18 years.
2 Combine effective collaboration with clear roles and responsibilities.
3 Consolidate institutional policy processes for effective change
4 Lead the next steps for Curriculum for Excellence with a long-term view.

The first three of these are then broken down into several complex sub-points, each elaborating on the sorts of changes that are needed to improve schooling in Scotland. Once again, allow me to at least attempt to translate some of the key points for the people who are not fluent in edu-babble.

The first recommendation calls for an update of some of building blocks of CfE, a clearer outline of what pupils should know and be able to do at different stages, and a radically transformed approach to assessment (with far less emphasis on exams) in S4–6. Recommendation number two suggests that it might be better if those in charge would actually listen to the people they always claim to be engaging with, and that we should be clearer about where responsibility lies for different parts of the system. In its third recommendation the OECD argues that we need to cut class contact time, gather better data (for example, by restoring the SSLN system that the SNP scrapped a few years ago), set up a proper national body to manage both the curriculum and assessment arrangements, and establish a programme (including a timetable) for reviewing the school system in future.

The final recommendation is the shortest but also perhaps the most cutting, because the OECD has felt the need to warn the Scottish Government that all of these changes need to be pursued together and that it should not cherry-pick the parts of the report it likes while ignoring the bits it does not.

Unfortunately, the government's immediate response was not at all encouraging. Their press release was headlined 'OECD review backs school curriculum' and went on to focus largely on the low-hanging fruit of replacing the SQA and removing school inspection functions from Education Scotland; there appeared to be little, if any, serious engagement with the extensive criticisms that the report presented. The decision to immediately foreground structural changes to the system's governing bodies was a transparently political one intended to keep the focus away from years of SNP policy failures that were now being exposed in a report that they themselves had commissioned. Questions must also surely be asked about the judgement of people (up to and including the First Minister) who had for so long backed organisations that are now, apparently, in desperate need of major rebuilding?

It is true that the government has stated that it will 'accept in full' all 12 of the OECD recommendations but their genuine commitment to the sorts of reforms that are so badly needed remains to be seen. A little more than 24 hours after the report was published, the education secretary announced that work to replace and reform the SQA and Education Scotland would be led by Ken Muir, a respected former head of the national regulatory body for teachers who is, nonetheless, undoubtedly from the heart of Scotland's existing educational establishment. Assurances have also been given that the Scottish Education Council will be reconvened, that a Children and Young People's Education Council will be established, and that the government 'will work alongside all partners to co-design a more detailed implementation plan on the OECD's recommendations' – but given that their first instinct was to spin the report to make them look as good as possible, and bearing in mind their track record, we should probably guard against too much optimism at this stage.

The problem is simple: if the OECD report is correct (and it is) then years of SNP policy have been wrong, and if things are going to get better then an honest recognition of that fact, and some apologies, are going to be required.

For us to make progress, the government would have to admit that they were completely wrong to impose standardised testing while scrapping the SSLN, and that doing so reduced rather than enhanced the quality of Scotland's education data. They would have to accept that they have failed to properly support teachers for at least the last decade, and that this has had serious knock-on effects for a whole generation of pupils. They would have to concede that they have been defending organisations and an exam system that are not remotely fit for purpose and should now be swept away. They would have to own their mistakes rather than blame others. And they would have to confront the fact that all of this has implications for the politician who insisted that she wanted to be judged on her record.

I am a long way from convinced that the people currently running the Scottish Government and the SNP are big enough or brave enough to do this, although I will of course be absolutely thrilled to be proven wrong.

Beyond Our Borders

It's easy to create problems, or make existing ones worse, by assuming that our way is the right way – just because something has always been so doesn't mean it wasn't a mistake in the first place or that it shouldn't be improved now. It is vital that we're willing to look to other countries and learn lessons from their successes and innovations.

However, the importance of context when looking around the world simply cannot be overstated. It would be easy, for example, to look at the PISA scores of nations like South Korea and assume that some feature of their school system must make it the blueprint for smarter, more successful children the world over; but doing so would neglect the undoubtedly enormous impact of a culture that sees school students engage in hours of private after school lessons extensive enough to support a multi-billion-pound tutoring industry. Likewise, some might assume that we in the developed and (allegedly) enlightened northern hemisphere have nothing to learn from approaches in the global south because we ignorantly and arrogantly dismiss the conditions within which their education systems operate.

What follows is a selection of features and ideas from different systems around the world. None are necessarily intended as recommendations (although they may well represent good ideas) but rather as snapshots of the very different ways in which other countries approach key aspects of schooling.

Finland

In educational circles Finland is a superstar, having been brought to widespread international attention following exceptional performances in PISA tests since the system commenced in 2000. This helped to draw attention to possible reasons for its success, such as the lack of private schools and the fact that children do not start formal education until the age of seven.

Another striking feature of their approach is that pupils in Finland are not subjected to any standardised testing, and do not sit any formal examinations, until they are reaching the end of their time at school.

Students sitting the matriculation exam face challenging, open-ended tasks far more complex that what you might typically find in a Higher exam paper. They must complete assessments in at least four subjects: a 'mother tongue' language paper is the only entirely compulsory component, with the rest selected from a range of options in the fields of languages, mathematics, and humanities and natural sciences. The tests are held twice a year and students can split them over up to three sessions (each lasting up to six hours) but may also complete them in a single exam period. Students are also able to resit failed tests twice if needed, ensuring that they are given a fair opportunity to perform at their very best.

Estonia

When countries around the world were struggling to adapt to the demands of online learning as a result of Covid-related school closures, Estonia was already well ahead of the curve. In 1996 the former Soviet state had set out to ensure that all schools had computers and internet access, a goal that was achieved just a few years later. Since then, the country has continued to focus on the use of technology 'for the benefit of social development'.

Since the beginning of the 21st century, Estonia has viewed internet access as a human right. This has resulted in a nation where almost all government services can be accessed online, but it also meant a focus on digital literacy, as well as technology-based learning and teaching resources that are now considered world-leading.

At school level, a national online library called the 'E-koolikott' (e-schoolbag) providing access to tens of thousands of centrally organised and approved teaching resources was already used in the majority of schools even before the coronavirus pandemic forced the switch to fully online learning.

Australia

Australia's federal system means that individual states have their own mechanisms for attracting, supporting and retaining teachers. In the state of Victoria, teachers can choose to defer 20% of their total salary for between one and four years (the 'work period'), and to then have this money paid to them in a subsequent period of sabbatical leave. For example, a teacher who completes a one-year work period would then be able to access more than ten weeks of sabbatical leave at 100% of their normal salary, or up to 13 weeks at 80%; at the other end of the scale, a work period of four years allows up to a full year of paid leave. Teachers may use these sabbatical periods to 'gain skills and experiences that they might otherwise not be able to access', but what they do with their time is ultimately up to them.

In Western Australia, teachers are offered significant support with housing and transportation expenses, as well as additional bonuses for working in 'remote' areas. An online calculator shows the level of assistance available for working in different regions and schools: someone applying for a job at Spencer Park Primary School in Albany, for example, can benefit from subsidised housing and free relocation, whereas a job at Jigalong Remote Community School comes with free housing, free relocation, an air-conditioning subsidy, and more than $20,000 in additional allowances.

Ireland

In the Republic of Ireland, although English is the universally spoken language across the country, the Irish language (or Gaeilge) is in fact the first official language of the state.

Some schools teach primarily in Gaeilge but even in English-language schools – which represent the majority of institutions – it is studied throughout the primary and secondary curriculum. Although pupils are able to secure exemptions, for example due to having additional support needs or because they have arrived in Ireland part-way through schooling, the formal expectation is that all pupils learn Irish throughout the entirety of their time at school. In terms of timetabling, Irish is regarded as equal to literacy and numeracy instruction.

The prominence of Irish in the education system is seen as a key policy for the protection and appreciation of the language itself, which is still used by a large proportion of people in some parts of the country but is spoken daily by only a small minority of the total population.

Colombia

In many of Colombia's rural schools, an educational model known as *Escuela Nueva* (New School), first developed in 1970s, is credited with raising standards and enhancing the educational experiences of some of the country's poorest children.

In schools following the model, students work from centrally produced learning guides, progressing through a range of individual and group tasks that allow them to work at their own pace both independently and collaboratively. When older pupils have completed their tasks, it is expected that they will assist their younger classmates.

But that doesn't mean that this a joyless, back-to-basics approach designed to grind pupils through a standardised curriculum – in fact, it is exactly the opposite. Escuela Nueva prioritises arts, expression, collaboration and social interaction amongst children, and is intended to create a co-operative, child-centred learning environment. Teachers also receive ongoing training to help maximise their skills.

Escuela Nueva was praised by the UN as far back as the early '90s for its impact in rural schools across Colombia and since then has been exported to numerous other countries around the world.

Singapore

In recent years, the tiny nation of Singapore in southeast Asia has attracted significant attention for its approach to preparing new teachers. Unlike in Scotland, where eleven different institutions offer teacher training (officially known as Initial

Teacher Education), Singapore has a single National Institute for Education. Here, the Initial Teacher Preparation programme develops the 'knowledge and skills required of teachers to competently meet the demands and challenges of a dynamic teaching career'.

As in Scotland, there are undergraduate and postgraduate routes into the profession, as well as another for O-level holders. In addition, there are more options for specialisation than are available in Scotland. Entry to teaching programmes is extremely competitive, at least in part because salaries are adjusted annually to ensure they remain in line with other professions.

New teachers must commit to at least three years in the classroom, during which time they benefit from mentoring from experienced colleagues. They are also paid 60% of a full teaching salary while training. Teachers in Singapore complete appraisals every year but are also entitled to one hundred hours per year of professional development activity – around three times the expectation in Scotland – and can pursue enhanced career paths such as master teachers, specialists or school leaders.

Tanzania

In Tanzania, the creator of a programme called the Jumuisha (Swahili for 'to include') Initiative hopes to help improve the experiences of children with special educational needs by supporting the development of their teachers.

An online library provides advice and information across four categories – hearing impairment, visual impairment, physical impairment and intellectual impairment – through a range of prompt questions. Teachers seeking support can use the library to access advice and information designed to help them work with students with additional needs, and they can also contribute ideas and approaches of their own, which are then quality checked before being shared with other educators.

The programme, which focuses on ensuring that teachers can easily access materials to help improve their classroom practice, won an African Union Education Innovation Prize in 2019.

Japan

When we talk about improving education, we often neglect the importance of having systems in place to help teachers improve the effectiveness of what they do in the classroom. In Japan, a model called jugyokenkyu (lesson study) exists to do just that.

A small team of teachers comes together to discuss a particular group of pupils and agree a specific area of need. They share their existing experience, analyse available data, access relevant research material and can even gain outside support. From this process comes a series of targeted lessons where one member of the group teaches, and the rest observe.

Each lesson is then, as the name suggests, studied by the group, with that analysis used to refine the next steps. At the end of the cycle the results of the project can be presented to a wider audience and, if successful, used by others.

Lesson Study is all about improving education by supporting and trusting teachers, and building a culture of professional improvement within and across schools.

International Baccalaureate

Although we can surely learn from looking at other countries, we should also be willing to learn from genuinely international experiences and expertise.

The International Baccalaureate (IB) operates in thousands of schools across roughly 150 countries. It is best known for the Diploma Programme (DP) aimed at 16–19-year-olds, although it also offers primary years, middle years and career-related programmes as part of provision for students aged 3–19.

DP students complete courses from each of six subject groups (studies in language and literature, language acquisition, individuals and society, sciences, mathematics, the arts) as well as the compulsory 'core' components: theory of knowledge, a 4,000-word extended essay, and 'creativity, activity, service' (CAS) projects.

Courses are designed to encourage an international outlook but allow for the specific focus of areas such as literature or history to be tailored to the country in which they are being used. The modular approach also provides flexibility and challenge, allowing students to pursue specific areas of interest including those that may be useful for university, college or employment prospects.

8

Building Back Better

SO FAR, I have tried to contextualise some of the past and illuminate some of the present of Scottish schooling. Understanding where the myths of Scottish education end and the reality begins, and interrogating what we really know about the strengths and weaknesses of the system, are vital if we are to hold leaders to account, recognise our blind spots and, most importantly, do the very best we can for our kids – but it all means nothing unless we are willing to make the sorts of big-picture changes that are really needed. Tinkering is easy but transformation takes more courage.

Schools may not be able to undo the effects of inequality, but they are not powerless, and there are things we could do to maximise their impact. In this chapter I am going to lay out a few ideas for reforming and improving the structures, practices and assumptions of Scottish schooling.

After the Pandemic

Almost since the pandemic started, and certainly since the first school closures as a result of rising infection rates, we have agonised over what to do with young people once it ends. In particular, we have witnessed massive anxiety over the idea of 'lost learning' and became so fixated on it that it we made serious mistakes with potentially long-lasting consequences. As we now begin to emerge from the crisis, and attention turns towards planning for the future rather than simply surviving the present, there is increasing pressure to succumb to a particular narrative around children's education: the need to make sure that they 'catch up' academically. This is, in many ways, quite understandable, but it is also misguided.

Examples of the catch-up narrative in action include calls for longer school days, shorter holidays, and national tutoring schemes. They all, to various degrees, misunderstand the problem before us. It might look like concern for kids, and those advocating such policies might even believe that to be the case, but in reality they are calling for us to protect the system and race back to a broken status quo, all while expecting those who have already suffered the most to do the hard labour that this would require.

It is – apparently – far too easy to forget that our kids have been through this hellish pandemic too. All that anxiety we've felt, all those times we've struggled to keep going, all those days when it just seemed too much: they've experienced it all as well. Those weeks and months without being able to see our friends or spend time with our extended families have affected even the most resilient children. Those with vulnerable relatives, or health conditions of their own, have lived in a state of constant worry, and every life lost has robbed a child of a grandparent, an aunt or uncle, a family friend, or even a parent.

But here's the thing: we're supposed to be the adults, which means that no matter how hard things have been, we should be the ones taking on the burden afterwards, not our kids. We shouldn't be demanding that young people work harder and harder to get things back to normal; we should be building a new normal around what they need. Anything less is simply a betrayal.

This is especially true given that the status quo to which some would have us return was, for far too many people across our country, a nightmare. We had constructed a system that not only failed to address systemic inequality but rather entrenched and at times even magnified it, and then told ourselves that it was a beacon of fairness and meritocracy. And now, when we have an opportunity to make things better, there are some who wish to see the poorest and most vulnerable put to work and forced to rebuild the very system that oppressed them.

The eventual outcome of the 2020 results scandal and subsequent improvement in areas like access to higher education showed that the system to which we are so attached is, after all, just like any other machine: people like us built it, and people like us can change it if we really want to. Remember that even within the confines of the existing (wholly inadequate) approach, pass marks and grade boundaries are already changed every year, and that the Scottish Government implemented an entirely new model of measuring success simply because it suited them to do so. It is entirely within our power to put our kids' mental health, personal development and overall wellbeing first. The issue is not whether we can change things – it's whether we can be bothered.

So instead of more hours in crowded classrooms, or expecting the poorest kids to spend their evenings being drilled through maths equations by private tutors, or demanding that teachers focus even more of their attention on mining just the right kind of data from their pupils, we should be looking at policies such as a massive expansion in outdoor and residential learning, fully funding a huge range of sport and social programmes, and making sure that those who need it can access counselling services within days instead of months or even years. We need to concentrate on our children's wellbeing above all, not their ability to perform all the same tricks and jump through all the same hoops as those who went through the system in pre-pandemic years.

Politicians have been perfectly happy to throw around soundbites about 'building back better' in the aftermath of this once-in-a-century catastrophe. Now they need to show that they actually meant it.

New Leadership Required

Although Scottish schooling is delivered by local authorities, the system is ultimately led by two key organisations that have come to dominate much of what goes on in classrooms across the country.

The first of these is Education Scotland, which was formed in 2011 through a merger between two separate organisations: Learning and Teaching Scotland, which was responsible for curricular materials and support for teachers, and Her Majesty's Inspectorate for Education, which – as the ridiculously pompous name suggests – was charged with inspecting schools in order to maintain standards. The second is the Scottish Qualifications Authority (SQA), which was also formed through a merger, this time of the old Scottish Examination Board and the Scottish Vocational Education Council. The SQA oversees an extremely wide range of qualifications, including the Nationals, Highers and Advanced Highers that make up the bulk of awards to school pupils in Scotland. It is, as a consequence, incredibly powerful.

In February 2021 the Scottish Parliament considered a motion declaring that neither organisation was fit for purpose. Despite the government's entirely predictable attempts to protect both bodies (and themselves), MSPs backed the motion by 65 votes to 58. In doing so, Scotland's elected representatives confirmed what many of those working in the education sector had already been saying for years.

Education Scotland has done little in its decade of life to suggest that the merger which birthed it was a good idea. Theoretically responsible for supporting classroom learning and maintaining overall school standards, it is regularly accused of effectively marking its own homework. Amongst teachers it is generally seen as ineffectual at best and a barrier to progress at worst and is often mocked (perhaps a little unfairly) as being a home for those who couldn't really cut it in the classroom but love telling others how to do the job through the medium of terrible infographics. Most of all, it is regarded as being simply too slow, clumsy and self-interested to actually support teachers. Nonetheless, its proximity to the Scottish Government, and the overall politicisation of Scottish education, means that it has not only been protected from serious accountability, but even rewarded for its failures, having for example subsumed the genuinely successful Scottish College for Educational Leadership and turned it into the in-house Professional Learning and Leadership team. Realistically, if Education Scotland had done its job over the last decade then this book probably wouldn't exist.

A change is most certainly required, and it needs to be structural. National teaching and exemplar materials to support the Scottish curriculum should probably come from one specialist organisation and always be made available in modern digital formats. Some of this could be sourced from existing material including that already developed by classroom teachers, while new resources could also be commissioned and developed from scratch.

Classroom support and teaching-focused professional development activity could be managed at a regional level, either through local authorities or the larger Regional Improvement Collaboratives that have offered questionable value since their creation. This might provide an opportunity for the introduction of expert teachers, who would be allocated lighter timetables in order to ensure that they are able to visit and support colleagues in other schools. Another option would be to invest public money in hugely effective teacher-led events known as TeachMeets, where professionals share ideas, resources and approaches with one another without the need for government interference or official control.

It would actually be better not to restore an organisation such as HMIE, and instead focus on inter-school collaboration as the primary means of assuring and improving standards, with support for this process, as well as an 'inspectorate of last resort' to deal with serious concerns, provided by an independent body with targeted expertise.

As with so much of Scottish public life, Education Scotland reflects the drive towards centralisation when the exact opposite is required. Rather than a single, lumbering organisation that tries to be a jack of all trades and ends up a master of none, and ends up far too close to government to be seriously accountable, schools would be better served by separate, focused, flexible bodies far removed from the political concerns of the government of the day, and with the expertise of working classroom teachers embedded at all levels.

There's no doubt that Education Scotland has failed to meet expectations, but the SQA has been even worse, with the coronavirus pandemic highlighting just how much damage the organisation (and by extension those running it) are capable of inflicting. In 2020, its unwillingness to trust teachers and a fundamental lack of concern for young people sparked the biggest school scandal of the devolution era – but while John Swinney was forced the apologise in parliament, those in charge of the SQA refused to accept that they had done anything wrong. The following year a new system was devised to cope with the cancellation of the exam diet and, once again, the SQA prioritised the protection of the system over the wellbeing of young people. All of this was simply a reflection of the arrogance and incompetence that characterises so much of the work done by an organisation which, without the slightest hint of irony, describes itself as being 'the heart of Scotland's world-renowned education system'.

For years teachers have complained that the SQA is entirely dysfunctional. Take, for example, the introduction of the new National 5 and Higher qualifications, when schools were provided with endless reams of vague and repetitive 'guidance' but just a single sample paper per subject. I was teaching at Arran High School when the new qualifications were being introduced and can still remember when the SQA dispatched an official for a meeting with our teaching staff. The idea, I presume, was to allay our concerns, but when this individual was asked why the SQA was refusing to produce more exemplar materials the response was that they were concerned that we would simply teach to the test. Not only was this an incredibly insulting thing to say to a room full of teaching professionals – my head of department made his feelings on that point absolutely crystal clear – it also showed just how little the SQA understood the actual process of teaching: by refusing to issue a proper selection of materials, the SQA made it more, not less, likely that teachers would feel the need to constrict their approach so that it remained within the boundaries covered by the single specimen paper.

There have been other examples too: petulantly expanding final exams with little if any concern for the consequences when internal assessments were removed; the decision to pursue qualifications and consultancy deals with countries guilty of horrendous human rights abuses; or the recent revelation that this publicly funded organisation was running a paid-for, results-boosting consultancy service largely used by elitist private schools.

The problem with the SQA is simple: it is run by, and therefore represents the interests of, all the wrong people. The current Chief Executive (at least at the time of writing) was previously in charge of the Scottish Government's Learning Directorate, while her predecessor had moved from a position at Scottish Enterprise. More than a quarter of the SQA board are 'management consultants'. There are no classroom teachers in the room when top-level decisions are made, nor does there seem to be any serious regard for the impact of those decisions on educators or their pupils. The starting point for reform of the SQA is therefore to completely rebuild its management system, placing genuine educational expertise, and a voice for young people, at the heart of decision-making. It might even be worth asking whether the collection of such a huge range of qualifications (including apprenticeships, SVQs, Highers, Skills for Work and HNC/HND courses) under a single umbrella has been a success.

Perhaps the biggest issue, and the one that actually helps to explain many of the other shortcomings, is that the SQA sees itself as the master of Scottish education rather than a servant. Until that fundamental arrogance is excised – a process that must begin with accountability for those who have overseen unacceptable failures – nothing else will make much of a difference.

In response to the recent OECD report into Scottish education, the government quickly confirmed that both the SQA and Education Scotland would be abolished. The former is likely to be reborn as an organisation overseeing both qualifications and the curriculum (on the face of it a sensible idea) while the latter will be replaced by at least two organisations, with inspection separated from classroom support once more. This could well be the starting point for some brave and much-needed reform, but it could also descend into little more than a regressive rebranding exercise. The Scottish Qualifications Authority could, for example, simply change the name above the door to the Scottish Curriculum and Qualifications Authority; responsibility for school inspections may be stripped from Education Scotland, but whatever remains, no matter its title, could easily be just as remote and ineffectual as the present incarnation. It is easy for the government to talk up changes to these powerful agencies, which is why they would rather attention was focused on this area than other aspects of the OECD report, but if the new bodies end up being run by and for the same sorts of people, based on all the old assumptions, and with one eye still turned to political concerns, then they will simply recreate the same sorts of bureaucracies and, ultimately, condemn us to the same sorts of failures. It's not just new names and faces that are required, but a completely new culture, and delivering it will not be easy.

Reform of the organisations running Scottish education is certainly a prerequisite for progress, but the need for new leadership goes even further than that. There is, as ever, a political angle as well.

When John Swinney was made education secretary in 2016, he was seen as the ultimate safe pair of hands. As Deputy First Minister, and after nine years serving as finance secretary, he was Nicola Sturgeon's most trusted ministerial big hitter. He was therefore tasked with sorting out some of the increasingly concerning problems in the sector by pushing through the government's priorities. Having turned education into *the* big political issue, Nicola Sturgeon needed a big political response. John Swinney was, first and foremost, the big political response. It must have made perfect sense in a meeting with the strategists and special advisers, but it meant that he was always the wrong person for the job.

It is scarcely credible to consider Swinney's time in post a success. Instead, it was marked by a series of embarrassing failures, the highest profile of which, at least until the summer of 2020, was being forced to shelve a flagship Education Bill when it became clear that attempts to push it through (despite widespread opposition to key proposals) would depend upon the support of the Scottish Conservatives. A historic pay deal for teachers was delivered, but the 13% increase was only agreed at the eleventh hour after the profession threatened massive industrial action.

As for that 2020 results scandal, the kindest possible interpretation is that the education secretary failed to grasp the basic details of the system he approved, despite being warned, over and over again, about what was coming. In this version of events, John Swinney failed to get his head around the numbers. The opposing possibility is that he understood the inevitable consequences of the algorithmic approach, but decided that discriminating against the poorest children (in an indirect but entirely obvious way) was an acceptable price to pay to protect the system. Maybe he trusted the wrong people, and I don't doubt that as he read the emails of devastated students from across the country and realised the human cost of his desire to keep the results 'credible', that he truly regretted his decisions.

But the truth is that by 2020 it was no surprise to see him get things so badly wrong: to be honest, the whole debacle felt like the culmination of the previous five years rather than a shocking aberration. People who worked closely with him seem to agree that he worked extremely hard and listened to what people had to say – but even if John Swinney is a good man, he was not a good education secretary. His time in post was, at best, just another wasted opportunity for progress; when he was finally moved on following the 2021 election victory, having clung on in the aftermath of the 2020 results scandal but never really recovered from it, the decision seemed like an act of kindness. The position is now held by Shirley-Anne Somerville, who was previously responsible for social security and, before that, served as the Minister for Further Education, Higher Education and Science. Whether this change in personnel signals any real shifts, either in policy or approach, remains to be seen, although the early signs have been less than encouraging.

For all Swinney's failures, however, we mustn't neglect to scrutinise Nicola Sturgeon's role in the policies and problems affecting schools in recent years. Her 'judge me on my record' speech was an act of naked politicisation of schools (and therefore children) for party advantage. By imposing standardised tests on children, the First Minister – a career politician with no teaching experience or expertise whatsoever – decided that she knew better than the teaching profession, and even as the plan to share the data fell apart, and the costs stacked up, she refused to back down, lest she be seen to suffer a political defeat. Her government has made it more difficult than ever to access clear and reliable information about the health of the Scottish education system. The attainment gap that she promised to close is going nowhere. We also shouldn't forget that while John Swinney was eventually sent out to take the heat for the 2020 results scandal, Nicola Sturgeon had defended the indefensible algorithm just as firmly (and arrogantly) and was also guilty of prioritising the credibility of the system over the wellbeing of young people. Time after time, she has seemingly put Scottish politics before Scottish pupils.

With the publication of the latest OECD report, it has once again been made clear that Nicola Sturgeon's choices have taken us in the wrong direction, with all the consequences and damage that this implies. These were political decisions, which makes them a political failure for which the First Minister is directly responsible.

Over the last five years Scottish schools have become increasingly politicised in no small part because those at the top have failed to provide the sort of leadership required, but they are not alone: the behaviour of many opposition politicians has been equally lamentable, and often even more so. Just as I finished writing this book, for example, Oliver Mundell MSP (the Scottish Conservatives' new education spokesperson) appeared in the press attacking updated national standards for teachers, having apparently found ongoing commitments to social justice and diversity particularly threatening. He whined to The Times that 'these unsubtle hints seem to have been influenced more by the SNP's agenda than Scottish values' in a grubby attempt to weaponise schools while appealing to his party's base. He even managed to include a reference to that mythical time 'when our education system was truly world-leading', just for the avoidance of doubt.

The need to build a new culture around Scottish schooling applies just as much to Holyrood as it does to the SQA or Education Scotland; for far too many of our elected representatives – those on both the government and opposition benches – the state of Scotland's schools seems to be, first and foremost, a matter of political advantage. It simply isn't good enough.

A New Deal for Teachers

In order to improve the quality of teaching in our schools, and therefore the pace and depth of learning amongst young people, we have to create the classroom conditions that will allow that to take place. After all, if we're not prepared to properly support their teachers, what does that say about our commitment to our children?

One of the most obvious and important goals for the improvement of Scottish education is therefore to have more teachers in our schools and fewer pupils in their classes, but progress in these areas needs to be dramatic if it is to achieve meaningful results. Reducing the size of a class from 30 pupils to 28 is going to make little, if any, difference to either the pupils or their teacher, but dropping from 30 to less than 20 could be a hugely positive step, albeit one that would also require the provision of additional classrooms, some new schools, and a lot more staff. Increasing the size of the teaching workforce would also help to address the increasingly concerning issue of teachers struggling to find work, or being forced to depend upon insecure supply posts that are really just zero-hours contracts by another name.

Limiting class sizes to 20 pupils at both primary and secondary level would take Scotland below the OECD average while ending the disparity between technical and non-technical subjects in secondary schools. Young people would enjoy more time with, and attention from, teachers who would find themselves with more capacity to really help their students.

But we also need to ensure that those increased teacher numbers and smaller class sizes are accompanied by another dramatic, and potentially transformational, shift: a significant reduction in class contact time. Teachers in Scotland spend more of their working week in front of their classes than almost any other nation in the OECD. Here, all teachers are expected to deliver 855 hours of lessons across the year, massively more than OECD averages for primary schools (778 hours), lower secondary (712), and upper secondary (680 hours). The 2020 OECD Education at a Glance report even uses Scotland as an example of a country with very high class contact time, pointing out that in the first years of secondary school, 'teachers spend 44% of their working time on teaching on average, ranging from 35% or less in Austria, Iceland, Korea, Poland and Turkey to 63% in Scotland (United Kingdom).'

Indeed, Scottish teachers' 'net statutory contact time' is exceeded only by Lithuania, the United States, Chile and, all the way at the wrong end of the scale, Costa Rica. So, while a pupil in Finland, Estonia, Poland, Japan, Iceland, Turkey, Russia and many others gets the benefit of a teacher with significantly more time to review their work, plan their next steps and generally focus on their individual needs, the equivalent Scottish child may find that their teacher, through no fault of their own, doesn't have the chance to give them all the help they require and deserve. Right now, our teachers are all too often working with one hand tied behind their back.

Teachers need to be spending less time in front of their classes. It may seem counter-intuitive, but it is the only way to create space for all the behind-the-scenes work – planning, marking, feedback, collaboration with colleagues, safeguarding, professional development and more – that is so essential to high-quality education. Our kids deserve a teacher with the time to do their job. The initial goal should be to achieve the OECD average before pushing to at least a 50-50 split between planning and teaching time. This would be a more realistic reflection of the balance of work carried out in schools and should ease the pressure that teachers currently feel to do huge amounts of work in the evenings and weekends, a culture which offers short-term benefits but leads to long-term burnout. The aim is simple: to give teachers more of the time and space they need to get on with their jobs.

Clearly, a reduction in both class sizes and teachers' contact time would require a significant and ongoing increase in teacher numbers across the country, but it could also open other opportunities to expand on what we think of as the teaching workforce. Could more music, PE, language and science specialists be provided for primaries, perhaps on a shared basis between clusters of schools? Might an expansion of outdoor and residential learning, or links with charities and community groups, or the provision of a wider range of vocational pathways and alternative qualifications, or even the incorporation of extra-curricular activities into the school day itself, free up time for teachers to concentrate on planning, development, assessment and, in the end, excellent teaching?

Cutting contact time so drastically might seem like a hard sell, especially if your main concern is politics rather than pupils, and it would need to be introduced gradually rather than in a single, headline-grabbing moment. Time, patience, dedication, commitment and, above all, trust would be required from a government that has generally shunned such ideas, and the (undoubtedly strong) urge to build new layers of control and bureaucracy in exchange for this additional time must be resisted, given that it would undermine the very premise of the

School Statistics: Annual Teaching Hours in Selected Countries
Source: OECD Education at a Glance

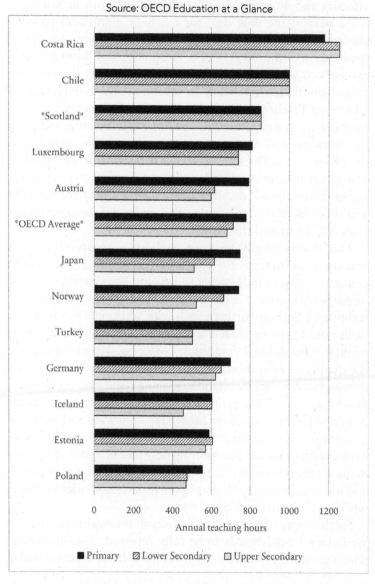

change in the first place: to allow teachers to make better, more effective and more professional use of their working hours.

As part of the new deal for teachers, significant funding should also be made available to develop options for career progression and professional development that do not require teachers to pursue promotions or secondments that remove them from their classrooms. In years gone by, a system called Chartered Teacher allowed experienced staff to secure a pay rise by engaging in a programme of professional learning, including the attainment of a Masters degree – but this approach was ditched in 2012. The scheme wasn't perfect, with one criticism being that it largely rewarded those with time and resources rather than skills and dedication, but the basic principle is sound and could be revived relatively easily, at least if the government were willing to find the cash.

The model might be improved by a greater focus on specialisation options for education professionals across the country, allowing individuals to develop their expertise either in particular subject areas or in broader fields like learning technology and supporting pupils with additional needs. These skills could then be shared with, and used to support, others in their school, local community or council area, enhancing the quality of education on offer while also expanding career development routes. Scotland's teaching regulator, the General Teaching Council for Scotland, already operates a scheme to recognise teachers who have engaged in significant and sustained professional development in areas such as outdoor education, assessment, numeracy, supporting new teachers, use of ICT and many more, but this needs to become a far more fundamental and universally accessible part of the progression offer for those working in Scottish schools.

Furthermore, the utterly disastrous shift towards faculties in secondary schools needs to be fully reversed. This approach, which grouped together several subjects under a single leader in order to save money on promoted posts, has not only robbed teachers of promotion opportunities but also diluted the support available to staff at all levels, placing a greater burden on teachers and, as a consequence, having a detrimental effect on the experiences of far too many pupils. Every department should be led by a subject specialist principal teacher at an absolute minimum, but serious consideration should also be given to restoring positions such as assistant principal teacher and senior teacher as part of the redevelopment of the vital support structures that have been so seriously undermined.

Finally, the pay structure for the teaching profession needs to be reassessed to ensure that we can attract and – crucially – retain the teachers that we need. At present, the starting salary for a teacher is around £27,500 and pay increases are applied over each of the following five years, settling at a salary of £41,500 per year. The problem is that, from this point, pay progression is only really available to those seeking promotions out of the classroom, despite the critical importance of experience within the teaching profession. A relatively straightforward way to reward continued service, and hopefully retain more experienced teachers, would be to introduce additional pay increases, perhaps at five-year intervals instead of the annual progression enjoyed at the beginning of a career.

Alongside the reduced contact time and class sizes, this could all help to ensure that teaching is properly recognised and supported, which in turn would lay the foundations for improving the educational experiences of young people in our schools. Improving teachers' conditions is the best way to improve the quality of teaching that happens in classrooms across the country. At the end of the day, isn't that supposed to be the point?

The School Starting Age

In recent years one fairly radical idea – at least for Scotland – has attracted increasing levels of attention and widespread support: changing the age at which pupils start school. Right now, children in Scotland start primary school at either four or five – but many believe that this should not happen until the age of seven.

Although we naturally assume that our traditional approach represents good sense and normality, the truth is actually quite different. Across the world, fewer than 15% of countries send their children to school aged four or five, and almost all of them have direct historical links to the UK through the British Empire. The overwhelming majority of countries actually send their children to school aged six, a full two years later than some children in Scotland head off to primary school, and there are more countries with a starting age of seven than there are those adopting the approach we simply take for granted.

What's more, there seems to be little rationale for our unusually young starting age beyond the fact that things have always been this way. If we were starting to build a public school system from scratch, how many of us would be arguing that the best place for a four-year-old child is a school classroom, or that they should be spending their time pursuing academic benchmarks rather than playing with their friends? Indeed, there are some very real concerns about the impact of sending children to school at such an early stage, with critics of the status quo citing the damage that can be done to young people's emotional and mental health when we try to force them through a system for which they simply are not ready. You can't force a caterpillar to turn into a butterfly and you risk doing a lot of damage if you try.

Those opposing change would perhaps argue that these concerns are outweighed by the outright educational advantages experienced by children in the UK – since they go to school earlier than their peers in other nations, they must also learn more and consequently outperform them? Not so. In 'top performing' countries such as Estonia, Canada and Finland schooling starts at six or seven years old. In New Zealand, parents can wait until their child's sixth birthday before sending them to primary school, a stark contrast to Scotland's approach where children begin school at the start of a pre-determined academic year. A 2009 review of PISA data found no evidence that starting school earlier led to increased reading levels by the age of 15.

Those pushing for change, such as backers of the Upstart Scotland campaign, argue that children benefit most from a play-based experience that aids their overall development, not a system that values measurable reading, writing and counting skills above all else. They also believe that a kindergarten system would help to ensure that all children benefit from play-based, pupil-focused learning, avoiding the current postcode lottery where some schools have adopted varying degrees of this approach (typically for their youngest pupils) while others have not.

One central principle behind implementing a play-based, ring-fenced kindergarten stage across the entire country is that it would protect children from the harms that can be done by a system that prioritises data and deadlines over wellbeing. Another is to help restore opportunities for active, social, outdoor play that are so crucial to children's all-round development. It's not that a kindergarten stage would, for example, mean that children would not learn to read until they start primary school at seven years old, simply that they would not be pushed to do so before they are ready in order to meet one-size-fits-all performance targets and curricular benchmarks. As any parent knows, during those early years children develop at markedly different rates and in entirely different ways: the one constant is that play and inquiry are how they learn. There is little if anything to be gained from ignoring these entirely natural variations, but there is increasing evidence that doing so can be damaging to young people's lifelong learning and wellbeing.

Like many people across Scotland, I have been convinced that raising the school starting age, combined with a revolutionary investment in developing a universal kindergarten system, is probably the ideal starting point for improving Scottish schooling – but the second part of that proposition is crucial.

If we want to do something about the injustices that manifest in the earliest stages of children's lives we should start, as the song says, at the very beginning, but simply sending children to school a couple of years later, while leaving the rest of our systems and approaches largely unchanged, would likely serve only to widen the divides between the richest and poorest families. By the time children reach two and half years old, measurable gaps between rich and poor have already appeared. One of the Scottish Government's own 'attainment gap' measures shows that more than 70% of children from the most affluent areas show 'no concerns' at their 27–30 month review, but that the figure for those from the most deprived areas is just 55%. More broadly, there is widespread evidence of massive vocabulary gaps between children from different social backgrounds by the time they are even toddlers, a divide that is driven by different early life experiences as opposed to innately different ability levels.

Sending children to school too early is only likely to exacerbate, rather than ameliorate, these issues. The development of a national kindergarten system, universally available to all children from the ages of three to seven, with mixed-aged groupings, and either massively subsidised by or entirely paid for through general taxation (just like primary and secondary school), would help to focus attention and resources on the vitally important early years. It is one of the very few policy changes that could begin to equalise the foundational experiences of children across

Scotland and taking such a step could be just the catalyst we need to rethink not just the school system but also some of our fundamental social assumptions.

Success would depend on both expertise and infrastructure. We would need to see the development of a well-qualified and high-status workforce and the construction of appropriate physical spaces (combining new or converted buildings with outdoor learning environments) across the country. In the end, the goal should be the creation of a truly national early years sector to replace the current patchwork of provision that further entrenches the divide between rich and poor. All of this would cost money, although given that we currently educate children from four years old anyway and are in the process of a significant expansion in early years provision, a lot of the resources are already likely to be in place.

This sort of change might also raise questions about the overall structures of primary and secondary schooling in Scotland. Just like with the school starting age, there is a tendency to believe that our current approach is also the ideal one, but what if we're wrong? If we were to raise the starting age of formal schooling from four or five to seven, would it then make sense to reassess the point at which children shift from primary school to secondary? Should we perhaps go further, and ask whether the introduction of a middle stage – such as those used in countries like the USA, Japan or Norway – might be more compatible with CfE and allow us to better meet the needs of young people? Maybe it would be better to alter our approach to the final years of high school so that those aged 16–18 learn in an environment that looks and functions much more like a college, thus ensuring that they are better prepared to take their next steps after leaving the school system?

There's really no reason why all of this shouldn't be up for debate, even if it means overcoming the small-c conservatism that so often dominates our approach to education. Sometimes it is worth asking how much of the status quo would be replicated if we were building a system from scratch and then using the answer to help us focus on the possibilities for progress rather than the limits of the present.

The biggest barrier to these sorts of structural changes is probably political. Although some aspects of early learning could be improved relatively quickly, especially given the recent publication of updated guidance for early years education in Scotland, there is absolutely no way that the entire landscape of Scottish education could be redesigned and rebuilt within a five-year window. These are generational changes for which no single government is going to be able to claim the credit, so why start the process at all? It is also worth bearing in mind that the chaos and anger sparked by endless, aimless animosity over schools suits some politicians just fine. Keeping people outraged is, after all, a more effective way of shoring up your vote (and keeping your job) than cross-chamber collaboration.

Changes on the sort of scale we require would demand the construction of a broad, forward-thinking, long-term consensus – to be blunt, it isn't clear that our elected representatives are up to that job. Perhaps they can surprise us.

Reforming Assessment and Certification

Even before the 2020 catastrophe there were plenty of people calling for a rethink of our approach to providing qualifications for school leavers. This is often discussed under the heading of 'exam reform' but that shorthand can actually be extremely unhelpful. It makes high-stakes, annual, end-of-year examinations seem like *the* crucial feature of the system, while also suggesting that any attempt to reform our approaches means a desire to 'abolish exams'. We should therefore be clear that we are talking about assessment and certification, of which traditional exams may or may not be a necessary feature.

The first thing to ask, though, is what is it all for? There are lots of different ways to generate scores and grades, but what is the goal that we hope to achieve? What we're really trying to do is identify and quantify some combination of the knowledge, skills, effort, progression and, ultimately, potential of young people, which sounds immediately complicated precisely because it is. We then have to issue confirmation of this process, such as exam results or school leavers' certificates, to enable (or ration, depending upon your perspective) progression to another stage of education, some form of training, or employment.

At present, the vast majority of Scotland's school leavers will have sat multiple exams in each of their final years of high school. National 5, Higher and Advanced Higher qualifications operate on essentially the same structure: one-year courses where grades are determined by performance in a final exam on a single day, with some subjects also incorporating a project or portfolio as a percentage of the overall result. The apparent strengths of such a system seem fairly obvious: everyone sits the same paper, on the same day, under the same conditions, ensuring consistency amongst all students, while anonymous marking and annual grade adjustments secure the credibility of the grades that are issued. By this thinking, our current system of final exams is incredibly fair to everyone. Except that it's not.

It is true that every student sits the same paper at the same time, but the idea that they do so under the same circumstances is a delusion, one built on the entirely false assumption that only the conditions inside the four walls of the exam hall have an impact on a student's test scores. But a student who got eight hours of sleep in a warm bed doesn't sit their exam under the same conditions as one who woke up cold during the night because there was no gas in the meter. A young person who starts the day with a healthy breakfast and a chat around the kitchen table isn't being tested under the same circumstances as one who had no time to eat because they had to make sure their siblings were ready for school. Pupils who walk into the exam hall thinking through their revision material are not being treated the same as the those who go in worrying about the health of the parent for whom they are a carer.

These sorts of divides are not even particularly extreme examples – they are the stories that play out every single year in every single school in every single part of the country. But we don't like to talk about it because the lie of the meritocratic exam system makes us feel better. We tell ourselves that the current system is fair because it is easier to believe the lie than confront the truth.

The high-stakes, make-or-break nature of the Scottish system demands that pupils perform to the best of their ability on a single day – less than 0.3% of a full year. It rewards those able to jump on command and punishes those whose circumstances mean that their best day might not happen to line up with a national exams schedule. This leaves our current approach inherently weighted towards those from more affluent backgrounds: those whose parents can afford private tutors, of course, but more broadly those who are just far less likely to be coping with emotional, psychological, social or family problems at any given time.

Pupils from the richest parts of Scotland are more likely to leave school with five Highers than the poorest are to leave with just one. Those wealthy pupils also have around a 40% chance of getting As for the Highers they sit, but for the poorest this falls to around 15% – indeed, in the final 'normal' exam year before the coronavirus pandemic brought massive disruption, young people from the most deprived tenth of Scotland were actually more likely to fail a Higher than get an A. We'd almost be as well just cutting out the middleman and giving grades out by postcode.

This is all absolutely fine if you think that wealthy kids are just smarter, harder working, more resilient, and have greater potential than poorer kids – but if, like me, you don't believe that, then it isn't hard to see why the 'exam system' as we know it has to go. The link between deprivation and educational development goes far beyond the exam system, of course, and it would be foolish to think that changing the way we test pupils could somehow demolish the great hulking edifice of structural inequalities that blight far too many lives. The whole point of being rich is to have advantages over others, both for yourself and for your kids, and no system, no matter how well designed, is ever likely to erase the link between affluence and attainment. We should not expect a certification system to untangle the deep threads of inequality running through society, but nor should we accept a system that is indifferent to that injustice or, at the most severe extremes, makes the situation worse. We cling to our existing approach not because it is fair, or even because it is accurate, but because it makes it easy to ration success and access in ways that maintain existing hierarchies and class divides. This has to change.

So, what should we do instead? First of all, we should be much more honest about the limits of our current approach even beyond its tendency to entrench the divides between rich and poor. We need to remember that the point of the system is supposed to be to certify attainment, progression and potential and ask whether the current model even achieves this. Is a student who leaves school with an A for Higher English, to take just one example, actually better than someone who gets a C or are they just better at passing the English exam? Does it actually make sense to award an A to the student who manages to perform well on one day, having scraped by all year, while a student who has been a consistent top performer but has one bad day is written off? Since 2014 there hasn't even been a proper appeals system for young people after the SQA abolished it. Does that sort of system ensure that we are rewarding those who deserve it, or identifying those best suited to a university place, or encouraging young people to exceed their own and others' expectations? I would argue that the answer is, very obviously, no.

In addition, it's worth remembering that it isn't just the way we generate the grades that could – and, many would argue, should – change, but rather the whole structure of certification for high school students. We need to be prepared to ask, and answer, some big and complicated questions.

Do we really need to grind young people through an annual testing cycle, or would it be better to switch to a system like Finland which waits until they are leaving school? By removing annual exams in fourth and fifth year, we would at a stroke free up a huge amount of time that is currently ploughed into prelims, study leave, coaching students through 'exam technique' and, of course, the actual exam diets themselves. If we're serious about giving students the best possible experiences and a world-leading education then surely those weeks, or even months, would be better spent actually teaching them?

Is there really any need to force all students to be assessed at a single point or could we instead provide opportunities that allow our students to be assessed when *they* are ready? Such a system works perfectly well in many contexts, including the incredibly high-stakes issue of the driving test, where a passing grade (no A, B or C here) permits us to hurl potentially deadly machines around at life-threatening speeds, so why can't it be applied to a high school maths qualification?

Do all subjects need to be assessed in the same way? In some areas a traditional style of final exam might be best, but in others it may be of no real value at all. Does it really make sense to use the same methods in English as we do in maths, art, music, physics, drama or computing, or is this just another feature of a system more focused on convenience and conservatism than validity or reliability? Are there even, perhaps, simply too many individual subjects, and might it be better to redesign the system to assess pupils' knowledge and skills using a modular approach within larger subject areas?

None of this necessarily mean there's no place for things that look and function like exams, especially if they are part of a suite of assessments designed to accurately reflect students' abilities, and no approach is ever going to be perfect. Systems that depend upon coursework can hand even greater advantages to those who can pay tutors, while those based on continuous classroom assessment can cause enormous workload problems that undermine the system from the other direction. There are always difficult balances to be struck.

For what's it's worth, here's the sort of system I would consider for English, the subject I have taught for the last ten years. Instead of a single qualification with a largely one-size-fits-all structure, I would introduce a subject area known as Literature, Language & Communication, which would offer a more flexible approach built on modules in key areas like literature (looking at different genres, eras and styles), communication (focused on conveying information), film and television, journalism, and even advertising. Each module could be made available at two levels – introduction and advanced – with students able to study whatever combinations are best suited to their strengths, interests and future plans, although all students would be expected to complete at least one literature and communication unit at introduction level. Rather than a one-year course, studies would continue over two or even three years, allowing progression in different modules as well as ensuring that students could be assessed when they are ready, rather than trying to force everyone through the same annual exam cycle.

At least some of every student's final grade would have to be determined by ongoing work throughout their studies, and in the case of those pursuing further or higher education in related fields I would introduce a dissertation that could be completed through a focus on any of the available modules, meaning that one student might complete theirs on a comparison of two pieces of classic literature while another looks at the development of print advertising or the way in which the internet has changed newspaper opinion columns. I would also retain a final assessment – this would, however, move away from the existing, Victorian approach and involve sittings across more than one day, with a range of resources available, and extended, real-world assessments tasks that stretch young people far more than the memory tests and hoop-jumping that define the current exams. This would all represent a pretty massive departure from the status quo but, for me, would vastly improve both the experiences of young people and the quality of work that they are able to produce.

The good news is that in the aftermath of the 2020 results scandal, and as we emerge from the pandemic, there seems to be greater pressure for reform than ever before. Political parties, teaching unions, parent groups, young people and even organisations like the Association of Directors of Education and the Reform Scotland lobbying group (hardly known for representing radical or revolutionary thinking) have called for some sort of change. Then again, it's always easy to say that things should be different when there seems little prospect of it happening; it is quite another to be willing to do the hard work to make it happen. The question we need to answer is whether we think our kids are worth the effort.

Getting to Grips with Technology

The emergency adoption of remote learning during the pandemic was far from an ideal testing ground, yet it did offer some valuable insights into ways in which schools could make greater use of the sort of technology that has already transformed society.

For example, if core lesson content (the material that is simply told or explained to the class, often on multiple occasions over the course of a year) is provided in video form then pupils are able to engage with it in a way that suits their needs: some may watch a video about semi-colon use, or the River Nile, or Pythagoras' Theorem once and take everything in; some will need to view it a few times, but will be fine after that; some will find it easier to watch in smaller chunks, pausing the video throughout to take notes. Young people could also access the material at a time and place that works for them and revisit the content as often as they like, making it accessible to those whose personal circumstances make normal school hours a challenge.

The ability to ask for help privately through direct messaging is also much more appealing for some students and thus encourages them to engage in exactly the sort of behaviour that enables them to develop and progress: they can identify areas of weakness and seek specific, individualised support from their teacher in order to improve, but don't need to do so in front of the whole class or even face to face.

Young people who miss periods of school due to chronic medical conditions or disruptive life events would also clearly benefit from having systems in place to allow their continued engagement in class, something which should not be beyond us in an age of fibreoptic and 5G broadband and near ubiquitous digital devices. This could mean lesson content provided on a tablet or laptop, but it could also mean the class being live-streamed and the absent pupil being able to interact in real time. Students with hearing impairments, or those for whom English is not their first language, could make use of the increasingly powerful but little-used live translation and subtitling technology that already exists, allowing them to enhance their understanding of classroom materials and their teachers' explanations where needed.

None of this should be taken as a suggestion that remote learning should or even could *replace* the classroom, or that we should necessarily be pushing to have young people learning from home as a matter of course; there are also big questions to ask about the impact of any shift towards a more tech-focused approach on teachers, who clearly could not be expected to provide both in-person and remote learning at once without major changes across the system to support it all. As we have learned (the hard way), blended and fully online models of teaching come with massive workload implications: even creating a short explanatory video for a relatively simple concept takes more time and effort than just standing up and talking about it.

Perhaps part of the solution to this problem would be for core material, or at least a great deal of it, to be created and distributed not by classroom teachers but rather at the regional or even national level, perhaps in a way that allows for individuals around the country to adapt some of the content to their own needs? Could a single national organisation with a specific remit create an extensive, evolving and adaptable online library of key curricular content, a Scottish e-Curriculum of sorts, to help teachers extract maximum value from modern technology? The work of bodies like e-Sgiol (initially set up to help address the challenges of providing education in the Western Isles) and the West Partnership during the disruption of the pandemic has helped thousands of pupils and teachers across the country and it would be absolutely absurd to throw away all the experience and momentum they have developed. Nonetheless, their use right now is primarily on an emergency model, a curricular triage unit for those in lockdown, all borne out of a crisis that is, we hope, now beginning to pass.

So, what do we do with all this work? We could just forget about it in our rush to get things back to normal, or perhaps keep it all online, but always as an add-on to what is presumably *real learning* that takes place elsewhere. Or we could try learning some lessons ourselves and work to make 21st century schooling for children a better reflection of the society in which they are growing up. The real prize could come from exploring and embedding the use of technology in teaching and assessment practices to actually complement and even augment what goes on in schools, and to broaden the horizons of young people. As I write this I am reminded of my son's reaction to a tabletop touch screen device at the brilliant Gairloch Museum, which allows visitors to learn about features of the area using a variety of media and interactive mapping technology. Virtual Reality devices are also becoming more powerful, available and affordable.

But turning any of this into a reality would require significant investment. Genuinely universal access to appropriate devices and broadband internet are non-negotiable prerequisites, but this is not the only issue: the skills and confidence gaps that exist, not just amongst pupils but also the adults who care for them, are a major aspect of Scotland's digital divide. Addressing this represents a huge challenge but also, perhaps, an equally tantalising opportunity: could a post-pandemic reimagining of the role of technology in education also be the catalyst for a revolutionary programme of digital upskilling across all of Scotland?

There's really no good reason why not.

Speaking Our Language

Most of this chapter is dedicated to changes that could improve students' learning environments and experiences, minimise inequality and maximise teachers' capacity, but there are other issues that run through schools and, ultimately, right to the heart of Scotland as a nation. One of those is Gaelic.

As pointed out in the Brief History section, the Scottish school system was very much a part of the state-driven campaign to marginalise and, ultimately, destroy Gaelic culture, but could it now help to protect and even restore it?

The language actually first appeared as a recognised subject in schools way back at the start of the 20th century, but it wasn't until 1999 that Sgoil Ghàidhlig Ghlaschu (the Glasgow Gaelic School), the first 'all-through' Gaelic institution, was opened. Since then, more and more young people have been able to enjoy the benefits of bilingual education in Scotland. According to the government, just under half of Scotland's 32 council areas now offer Gaelic Medium Education (GME), although some have arrangements with neighbouring local authorities to ensure provision. Around 60 primary schools are involved in GME, which represents just 3% of the total number of primary schools across the country. A relatively small number of secondary schools also offer education in Gaelic.

In GME, pupils learn solely in Gaelic in primary 1 and primary 2, with English then introduced from primary 3 onwards. This immersion approach is intended to help develop children's connection to, and confidence with, Gaelic from the very earliest stages of their education.

In 2020, official statistics showed that 4,846 pupils (approximately 7% of the total number) were being schooled in GME. This represents an increase of around 50% on the 2015 figure and is more than eight times the number now recorded as speaking Gaelic as their 'main home language'. There is absolutely no doubt that there is plenty of demand for GME, but it's not all good news: the number of pupils across the country in Gaelic learner classes dropped in the same five-year period, falling from 6,745 in 2015 to 5,712 in 2020. When we focus on the exams data available for s4–6 students the picture becomes even more grim, with both Gàidhlig and Gaelic Learners attracting fewer students than almost every other subject. In 2020, a grand total of 130 pupils in Scotland attempted Higher Gàidhlig and just 62 studied Higher Gaelic Learners. The figures for National 5 level were 183 and 125 respectively. As it stands, only five exam subjects are available in the Gaelic language: geography, history, modern studies, maths and applications of maths. The latter is a relatively new subject while the other four are the same ones first offered in Gaelic way back in 1993.

It's clear that serious attempts are being made to protect and even expand the language, and that we have seen at least some progress, but it has been painfully slow. Part of the problem, of course, is the ignorance and – let's call a spade a spade – bigotry of what you might charitably (but still with suitable disdain) refer to as the 'anti-Gaelic crowd'. You know the ones: those who insist that Gaelic is a 'dead language' or regard it as a relic of a backwards way of life, or who spit out 'Gaelic was never spoken here' whilst driving home to Milngavie, Ardrossan, Dumbarton, Wemyss, Polmadie, Dundee, Banff, Airdrie, Corstorphine, Dumfries, Cumbernauld, Monifieth or any number of other places. They're the people who think that all of Scotland should look, and sound, like their Scotland. In their world, a bilingual road sign provokes a surge of equal parts fear and fury (such people clearly shouldn't be allowed behind the wheel) and a bit of Gaelic on a public document is a sure sign that society as we know it is about to be destroyed.

It's all idiotic, of course, but it isn't new or even especially rare – these views, which are widespread, socially acceptable and even boosted by some politicians and parts of the media, are just another example of a long-standing prejudice that has afflicted Scotland for generations and which manifests in all sorts of ways. It is one of the very worst features of our country.

Whilst travelling for my first book, *A Scottish Journey*, I was lucky enough to spend a night on Skye's Waternish peninsula. I stayed with Shaz and Ali, owners of Mint Croft, who shared with me a document entitled *Waternish: Place Names and Associated Lore*. It was written as a dissertation by local woman Kathleen MacLeod, who used the knowledge of Gaelic speakers from the area to meticulously catalogue the origins of, and the stories behind, the remarkable variety of place names on just that single stretch of land. For example, one location is known as An Talamh Fhuar, which means 'the cold ground', so named because local people were moved there against their will in order to hide their living conditions from wealthy visitors who had come to the area for hunting and fishing. If Gaelic ceases to be a living language, these sorts of stories, their place in our history, and the links to our ancestors, would be lost and our country irredeemably impoverished.

To make matters worse, these issues are magnified by attitudes towards other languages in general. We don't – or at least shouldn't – value, respect and teach languages because we expect our kids to need to speak one for work or on holiday a decade or two down the line. Teaching Spanish, for example, isn't about making sure you can shout *doz cervazas por favor* while staggering around Magaluf. That soulless, strictly transactional view completely misses the wealth of knowledge, self-confidence and cultural understanding that can be gained from learning languages, foreign or otherwise.

Let me give you an example. In the Canary Islands, to the west of Tenerife, lies La Gomera, a beautiful island that is smaller than Arran and has a population of fewer than 25,000 people, putting it roughly on par with towns like Bishopbriggs or Renfrew. If you've been to places like Los Cristianos and Playa de las Americas, it was the shadowy rock hovering on the horizon, but most people who have seen it from a distance have never actually visited. The stunning Garajonay National Park – an extraordinary laurel forest that is one of the last remnants of an ecosystem which once covered much of Europe and northern Africa – is recognised as a UNESCO World Heritage Site. There's plenty of human history too, such as Christopher Columbus' ships making their last stop there before heading across the Atlantic to 'discover' America. But La Gomera has another, arguably even more fascinating, claim to fame: a unique whistling language known as Silbo Gomero (or simply El Silbo) that is also recognised by UNESCO, this time as part of the Intangible Cultural Heritage of Humanity.

Before the days of modern roads, infrastructure and technology, Silbo was a vital means of sharing information across the steep gorges and jagged peaks that define the island, and although it is no longer necessary as a form of communication, and despite the fact that almost nobody outside of La Gomera can understand any of it, Silbo has been a mandatory part of schooling on the island for more than two decades. The reason for this is simple: it is regarded as an important part of Gomeran history and culture, something vital and valuable and to which the island's children are entitled. All of that is, or at least should be, true of Gaelic in Scotland.

With all young people in our country expected to learn a second language from the start of their time at school, it seems obvious that it should be Gaelic, with another 'foreign' language such as French, Spanish, Mandarin, Urdu or Arabic then introduced from primary 5. Pupils should study Gaelic throughout their 'broad general education', from primary 1 all the way through to the end of s3, both as a subject in its own right and as part of cross-curricular work that links different subject areas together. Gaelic courses and qualifications should also – obviously! – be available in every single school (and college) in Scotland.

In order to achieve any of this, however, we would need teachers. Lots of them. When you speak to people working in GME it quickly becomes clear that the biggest barrier to its continued expansion is not demand but supply. The lack of staff is holding Gaelic teaching back and there is no doubt that extensive training and recruitment programmes, with plenty of political and financial backing, are required. Already qualified teachers should be able to learn Gaelic as part of their professional development work, with support available for this to happen within the working day rather than viewing it as a bolt-on to be completed in the evenings or at weekends.

Furthermore, a concerted effort should be made to attract Gaelic speakers into the teaching profession: grants such as the £20,000 bursary for those seeking to teach subjects like maths, physics and computing should be made available, and consideration should also be given to waiving the need for an undergraduate degree when native and long-term speakers of the language wish to become teachers of it.

But even these changes, which would take significant time, commitment, and resources to achieve, aren't really enough if we want to do more than make Gaelic a curricular box to be ticked. Gaelic in every school would be great, but it needs to be part of a broader push for Gaelic in society.

One particular area on which we should focus is, as ever, the early years. In Comhairle nan Eilean Siar (where Gaelic language teaching is now the default option for pupils starting primary school) a renewed focus on Gaelic in pre-school education is evident through the ongoing re-establishment of 'Parant is Paiste' (parent and toddler) groups. Supported by early years officers and even Gaelic tutors, such groups not only introduce children to the language at the earliest stages, they also support parents in developing their own understanding and confidence. In doing so, the idea is to increase young people's exposure, ensuring that the language can move beyond their classroom and into their living room.

As with poverty and deprivation, it is absurd to expect schools to solve what are clearly social challenges surrounding Gaelic, and even the introduction of mandatory classes in schools would not, in and of itself, be enough to rescue, protect and expand the language and its associated culture. Nobody can reasonably expect schools alone to arrest and reverse centuries of imposed decline. Nonetheless, Scotland's school system was one of the tools used to attack Gaelic and, having been part of the problem for so long, it doesn't seem unreasonable to ask what must be done to make it a part of the solution.

9

Conclusions

OVER THE COURSE of this book I have attempted, hopefully with some measure of success, to cut through all the noise that surrounds education and help you to get at least a little closer to the truth about Scottish schools.

I have told the story of Curriculum for Excellence, which began with lofty and undoubtedly noble ambitions but lost its way early on, has never recovered, and may have now been fatally undermined. I have offered a more complete interpretation of some of the key data than you'll find in newspaper reports (including my own) or political speeches. I have examined the attainment gap narrative that has come to dominate debates about schools without ever making things better for the poorest pupils. I have provided a blunt and, at times, necessarily scathing assessment of how the system responded to the challenges of the coronavirus pandemic, despite the very best effort of teachers, parents and young people.

I have also tried to highlight a small selection of the enormous range of good news stories emerging from Scotland's schools, because for all the curricular problems and political failures, we mustn't forget that Scottish education remains excellent, or that those working in schools up and down the country do extraordinary work on a daily basis as they strive to do the very best for our children. Finally, I have offered just a few suggestions for what we might do next.

And there was so much that I left out. Sections offering a

detailed deconstruction of shoddy school league tables, or an explanation of why setting by ability is such a bad idea, didn't make the cut, and there are entire spreadsheets full of government and SQA data that have gone untouched on this occasion. As I wrote in the introductory chapter, many of the sections of this book deserve an entire publication of their own: I'd love to read a book about the experiences of minority ethnic pupils and teachers in Scotland, and another about the impact of the school system on Gaelic life, and another about the different views and experiences of the so-called 'inclusion agenda', but I'm clearly not the best person to write them. More can also be done to demystify the actual processes of teaching and assessment for parents, pupils, politicians and policymakers.

If, in the process of writing this book, I have reached one central conclusion, settled on one core truth that we must accept, it is this: more than anything, we need much more honesty about the sources of the problems in our schools. If we are to have any chance of seriously improving either our approach to education or the lives of those who always seem to be left behind, then we need to be willing to tell the truth.

I would love to tell you that different school structures, a new approach to preparing teachers, a particular reform of certification systems, or a grand combination of all of this and more, can change everything. I absolutely understand why people want to believe that everyone is equal inside the walls of our schools, and that once there every 'lad and lass o pairts' can transcend the circumstances from which they came. I want to believe it too. Everybody *wants* to believe it. But it isn't true.

The challenge of improving Scottish education largely comes down to two key factors: the equalising impact of the classroom and the intersectional effects of social class. The problem is that we assign too much weight to the former and wilfully ignore the latter.

Back when I was teaching on Arran I came across a statistic

that has always stuck in my mind. In England, one of the most common measures of a school's success and effectiveness has traditionally been the number of pupils gaining 'five good GCSEs'. But according to Professor Dylan Wiliam of the University College London's Institute of Education, 'only 7% of the variation between schools on this standard benchmark is due to the effect of the school. The other 93% is due to factors over which the school has no control.'

Ninety-three per cent.

It rather puts the whole 'closing the attainment gap' schtick into perspective, doesn't it? Even if schools' level of influence were two or three times as strong as suggested, the impact of other factors (for which read social and family background) would remain overwhelming. And remember that none of the recent, headline-grabbing attempts to 'close the gap', from standardised tests to a £120m funding pot, were launched from a standing start. Politicians and commentators may have only recently woken up to the reality of educational inequality, but the rest of society has already spent generations learning how to maximise the socioeconomic power of universal, comprehensive schooling, and squeeze whatever advantages can be found from its limited overall influence.

Of course, we can still do more. Smaller classes and lower contact time, a properly honest appraisal of Curriculum for Excellence, better use of technology and a new approach to end-of-school certification are just a few of the sorts of changes that would help to improve young people's experience of schooling. What's more, we should always be looking for ways to minimise the inequality of experiences between the richest and poorest students (or *closing the attainment gap* if you still prefer the buzz-phrase) and we can certainly do more to reduce the costs of schooling for families across the country.

Additional charges for certain subjects are an affront to the principles of universal education and should never have been tolerated. Free school meals should be expanded so that schools offer a free breakfast and lunch to all pupils. If uniforms are to continue then the trend must be towards generic, flexible, affordable and culturally inclusive choices. Every single child should have the opportunity to learn *at least* one instrument for free and to a standard that is at present only possible through private tuition. Some of this was promised in the most recent SNP manifesto and a deal between the government and councils to end charges for various subjects and music lessons has recently been announced, but time will tell whether this truly represents a much-needed reassessment of our priorities or just the latest political sleight of hand.

All pupils should also be entitled to at least two fully funded outdoor and residential trips in both primary and secondary school. This would not only guarantee universal access but also embed the importance of such experiences for young people. Following the same principle, we should seriously consider a similar commitment to foreign travel, promising that every single secondary pupil will be able to visit another country before leaving school. My own experience of this – a month-long trip to Australia that included time spent with two different Aboriginal groups – was life-changing, but the cost of such things leaves them entirely out of reach for far too many families.

The need to overhaul the data we collect is also pressing. Often questionable at best and misleading at worse, it regularly fails to reveal the truth about schools whilst also exerting perverse and debilitating pressure across the system. An expanded SSLN should be restored to replace ACEL data for national reporting of standards at primary and lower secondary, with the failed standardised testing system ditched as well. Both attainment and destination data need to go beyond the current crude framework to reveal in greater detail the reality of the gaps between rich and poor pupils; the same is true of, for example, university application and entrant data.

And of course no discussion about improving the quality and equalising power of education would be complete without a mention for Scotland's private schools. These elitist organisations are undeniable engines of social inequality – that is, after all, the whole point of their existence. They sell social segregation rather than a superior education, charging thousands and thousands of pounds per year for their product. Private schools allow the wealthy to purchase even greater privileges, and even deeper connections, for their kids and further distort our society in the process. It's simple: public education exists to mitigate inequality whilst private education exists to protect it. Stripping places like Hutcheson's Grammar (which charges up to £13,000 a year) and Fettes College (with fees of more than £30,000 a year) of tax breaks associated with charitable status is a welcome move, although the very fact that such institutions masquerade as charities is, itself, an insult. Ultimately, however, Scottish schooling, as well as Scottish society as a whole, would obviously be much improved by the abolition of fee-paying education.

But even if we do all of this and more, massive injustices will persist at every level, precisely because those injustices do not originate in schools and cannot, therefore, be solved by them. The 'attainment gap' is a function of socioeconomic and political failures rather than shortcomings on the part of schools – it is simply what massive intergenerational inequality looks like when viewed through the prism of education data. It is true that over the last decade some of the gaps between rich and poor have been narrowed (at least if you find the right way to measure them) but the fundamental inequalities in experiences remain. Yes, we have opportunities for improvement, particularly where we replace systems and assumptions that entrench inequality with those that might instead mitigate it. The problem is that there's just no changing the fundamental equation, which in the end is actually very simple: injustice in equals injustice out.

When we tolerate social evils such as poverty, homelessness, alienation and isolation, gender-based discrimination, racism, homophobia, transphobia and much, much more – because doing anything about them means having to change how we live – we ensure that they will be reflected in our schools.

If you want to improve schooling outcomes then you need to improve peoples' lives, but if you just keep on feeding enormous inequality into the education system then you shouldn't be surprised when it generates much the same imbalances at the other end.

Injustice in equals injustice out.

So, if people are really serious about addressing educational inequality, 'closing the attainment gap' and 'building back better' they also need to be serious about a range of radical and redistributive social policies. Progress in areas such as housing rights, employment law, welfare, violence against women, tax reform, healthcare, public transportation, anti-racism, climate justice, the care system, accessibility, LGBTQ+ inclusion and even land ownership could transform educational experiences, and life chances, in ways that school-focused policies will never, ever achieve.

Both our school system and our society have had long-standing failings mercilessly exposed by the Covid pandemic. The crisis has shone a fresh light on all sorts of deep-seated injustices which we had ignored or tolerated for far too long: think of the way in which the inadequacy of the exam system was exposed, or the fact that rough sleeping was virtually eliminated after years of indifference and inaction. These have been the hardest times of our lives, times which far too many people did not live to see, but as the storm finally begins to pass, we have a choice to make: do we look backwards, and spend the next few years rebuilding the old bad world? Or do we take this opportunity to work together and build something better?

I think we should do the latter: even though it's harder; even though it means admitting that mistakes have been made; even though it will upset all the people invested in the status quo.

But how do we begin what will undoubtedly be a complicated and lengthy process? Well, we're going to have to talk. We don't need another national debate but rather a national conversation, one that values the voices of pupils, parents, teachers, academics, voluntary groups, businesses and more. Led either by an independent panel or, even better, a citizen's assembly, such an initiative could bring together ideas and insights from every community in Scotland as well as further afield. Crucially, it could also refresh and depoliticise the democratic mandate for fundamental, maybe even radical, reform of our schools.

The pandemic has been devastating but it has also provided us with an opportunity, if only we are brave enough to grasp it. The time has come to take stock of where we are, with an honest assessment of how the whole system works and, perhaps above all, who it works for, because it is only in doing so that we can give ourselves the chance to construct a better future for our children.

We need to ask what we think our schools, and our education system as a whole, are actually for. Is the goal to mould our kids into productive workers or well-developed human beings? Are we more concerned with positive headlines and boosting CVs or with finding out what really works? Is the priority to generate ever-improving test data and exam grades or are we actually interested in enhancing the experiences of young people at every stage of their development?

How should we structure Scottish schooling? How do we give teachers world-leading working environments that allow them to maximise their own impact and help their students achieve their full potential? How do we ensure that all pupils and their parents have the support they need? What will a reformed curriculum look like and how will assessment work? How do we attract, and retain, the 'best and brightest' into the teaching profession? How can we gather data that tells us what we want to know in ways that does not distort the classroom experience? What steps do we need to take to tackle misogyny, systemic racism and all other forms of conscious and unconscious discrimination that continue to blight the lives of far too many children and adults in schools?

And perhaps most importantly, how do we keep the petty partisan squabbles of bickering politicians away from our kids?

All of these questions need to be answered if promises to 'build back better' are to be realised. Some of these discussions will be uncomfortable because they will, inevitably, force us to recognise the areas in which we have all fallen short – but the alternative is that we continue to fail thousands and thousands of children every year. That can't be an option. Not anymore.

We must do better and I truly believe that we can, but most of all I believe that our children deserve better than a society that is too afraid to try.

More Ideas for Improving Scottish Schools

As soon as I started writing this book I knew that I wanted to include more voices than just my own, so I set up an online form where people could submit their ideas for improving Scottish schools. I thought I might get a few dozen responses but ended up with hundreds.

Proposals such as reforming exams, increasing additional support needs provision and reducing class sizes were particularly common, as was an increased school starting age. Some suggestions were fairly technical (like changes to initial teacher education courses) while others, such as calls for greater support for young people experiencing trauma, were much more personal.

Although I have only been able to publish a selection of the suggestions that were submitted, it is clear from even this small sample that there is no shortage of ideas for improving Scottish schools.

Teachers

ASN provision is woefully inadequate. We need training for ASN teachers (I am one and receive no formal training unless I pay for it myself). Additional pay for the role is needed if additional training is to take place – it prevents the role being seen as a cop out or easy job and gives an alternative to classroom teaching for those who'd wish to progress.

Increased ASN funding is essential, with the ability to operate a hybrid model within schools: specialist provision plus well supported mainstream. The current inclusion model does not serve all children well at all and is simply the money saving option. I'm for inclusion in principle, but it has never been adequately implemented or funded. Classroom assistant posts are some of the lowest paid roles in education – their job is complex and deserves to be renumerated accordingly.

Leslie-Anne

End multi-level teaching in schools. I'm currently teaching N4 – Higher in the same class. Not enough teacher time is being directed to each course and the students are suffering for it. This is key to closing the poverty related attainment gap.

Joanne

A class size maximum of 15 at ALL stages in primary and secondary. This gives more time for each pupil, allows seamless movement from individual to group to class teaching, delivers better achievement levels for each pupil, gives teachers better balance between teaching and preparation, develops closer connections amongst pupils, and gives confidence to those otherwise lost, unnoticed or intimidated by larger grouping.

Katherine

Many options came to mind: reduced contact time, smaller class sizes, a true spread of assessment across the year. However, as a secondary teacher I kept coming back to the return of department heads and teacher classrooms. Department heads are leaders specialising in that subject, who have experience and skills and are remunerated as such. Faculty heads seem to 'deputise' non-promoted staff to do tasks which would be in their remit if they had the knowledge to do them. As for classrooms, teachers having their own room allows them to always be there waiting for the next class. This sets a tone immediately and helps calm any disruptive behaviour before it might start. It gives a sense of ownership of the space to both that teacher and the classes they teach.

Paul

Ban private schools. It is the elephant in the classroom with regards to equality of opportunity and undermines the notion of Scotland as a country where achievement is based on merit. If private schools do not provide an advantage, then they are pointless (and can be abolished as such); if they do provide an advantage, they are an instrument of privilege (and should be abolished as such). For a serious and tangible impact on Scottish society, this should be the first move in education.

George

Not the flashiest idea, but I would make literacy a bigger part of Initial Teacher Education (ITE) for secondary teachers. When I qualified we were told that literacy was 'the responsibility of all' but we never really learned why or how to implement it. My experience as a literacy coordinator has shown me that teachers are very keen to learn effective strategies but that CPD can feel like a bolt-on. The ability to teach reading, writing, talking and listening should instead be an integral part of what it means to be a teacher. To achieve this, I'd like to see a literacy module in every ITE programme. Students would first learn general approaches before exploring how literacy works in their subject discipline. This would make it easier for pupils to access every subject and (according to recent research) help us close the poverty-related attainment gap and ease P7–S1 transition. I'd add that literacy needs this more than numeracy because it affects every subject to such a great extent.

Jonathan

We could stop this culture of launching from one great initiative to another in order that another box can be ticked. For those of us who have been teaching all our adult lives it is utterly soul destroying – these faddy things don't work and they don't stand the test of time. And heaven help you if you dare to challenge any of these initiatives – there is no scope for people in Scottish education who genuinely want to discuss, challenge and improve. Those who go far and get promoted accept all of these initiatives and try to make them work when surely they know in their soul they are doomed to fail and are little more than a flash in the pan.

Kerry

Getting rid of presumption of mainstreaming and replacing it with true inclusion. The former is a cash saving exercise, a way to include ASN kids who are often not interested in exams (as that's the only way we know how to assess) and has nothing to do with meeting the needs of all of our children. ASN schools are worthwhile places, most of them do good work

Livvi

A more whole-hearted approach to outdoor learning, including residential experiences for all young people regardless of their socioeconomic status. Learning outdoors is something that is often seen as 'fluff' in education, something that is nice but has little real merit: there isn't an Higher in exploring the outdoors after all. However, outdoor learning is often a stepping stone for all of us, not just students, to discover a huge amount about ourselves and what is important to us. Even simply the opportunity to be outside and being exposed to the natural world is of huge benefit to everyone's mental health, and that alone makes embedding outdoor learning more fully in education important. And this still ignores the other possible benefits like learning more about conservation, biodiversity, etc.

In addition to this the opportunity for all students, not simply those who can afford it, to have residential experiences both nationally and internationally is important. These experiences give young people vital time to help shape their own identity, build relationships with their peers and to explore activities and parts of the world that are of interest to them. It is no coincidence that if you ask someone about their fondest memories of education residential experiences rank very highly. These experiences need to be available more often, and I would notionally suggest twice in primary and two/three times in secondary education, and must be made available to all by seeing local authorities given the resource to provide these opportunities for free to all.

Brian

Allow teachers to actually teach rather than making them spend countless hours in pointless meetings and useless CPD events/school improvement groups to just tick a box to meet the council/government agenda. We are told we have to join groups to meet the school improvement plan. I have been teaching 8 years and not one initiative has been successful or had any positive impact on the pupils in my class. Utter waste of time. I am so fed up spending all my time attending these when it could just be communicated via e-mail.

Emma

I believe that the Scottish Parliament, not the government, should be held accountable for Scottish Education. Education has become so politicised and is now often used as a stick for one party to beat the other with, and so there seems to have developed a culture of 'fear of failure' in which the government and the main bodies (Education Scotland and the SQA) are completely unwilling to admit that there may be anything wrong in Scottish education. This stifles creativity and lends itself to a 'command and control' agenda. The current Education and Skills Committee is there to hold the government to account but seems to be quite toothless in that it cannot force through any change or have any significant impact on policy. If this committee was given more decision-making powers then all parties would have to come to a consensus on the direction of travel and there would be less political point-scoring and a vested interest from all sides in making Scottish education better, rather than looking for cheap jibes that can be levelled at each other through the media or in the debating chamber.

Kennie

There is an urgent need to change the approach to assessment at a fundamental, philosophical and structural level. The current approach has mutated into a technocratic process that treats learners as little more than data sets to be mined, categorised and sorted. And for what purposes? Firstly, it seems, to provide a justification for the very system that carries out this dehumanising process. And secondly, to provide a mechanism to assign selected learners entry to Higher education courses based on the value the system ascribes to the data they produce. 'The algorithm' was already firmly embedded into Scottish education well before the results crisis in 2020.

Dean

Promotion of inexperienced staff must stop. Staff should have to teach for a minimum number of years before being considered for leadership. This would ensure they have experience both of dealing with pupils but also of working with colleagues as equals. Too many people are racing up the career ladder to 'leadership' when what we need are good, committed teachers. There's no reward for this other than job satisfaction but too often it is overlooked as an acceptable choice.

Jillian

Class sizes should be limited to 20 with two adults per class as a minimum. With the presumption of mainstreaming, more and more children with additional support needs are being let down through the simple fact that they are placed in a mainstream school with teachers who through no fault of their own don't have the skills to support them. There isn't enough man power or time in a day to properly get it right for every child. It's a final balancing game for a teacher to play: direct all your focus on the two or three children with support needs to allow them to access the curriculum whilst not supporting the 25 others in your room, or spend your time with the class furthering their education whilst letting down the children with additional needs. Each individual school or teacher could not possibly have the range of knowledge or skills required to replace that which has been lost by the closures of specialist provisions. Teachers work so hard to make sure every child in their class is achieving, but with 20 plates spinning, eventually one is going to drop. Perhaps if the Education Secretary had actually spent time in a school (by that I mean working in a setting, not attending as a pupil) and understood this, things would surely improve?

Jenni

Class sizes. When I first started at my current school infant classes were capped at 18. I had three years in a row teaching P2 with 16 pupils each year. I knew each and every one of those pupils so well – both academically and socially. I had children with high levels of need but could support them well due to the small numbers. I am currently in my 4th year in a row teaching classes of 32 or 33. There is a very wide range of abilities within my current class and it is impossible to meet all of their needs. There are some pupils I do not know well at all. There is zero space in the room and we don't even have a proper library area. I do not believe the current government will ever cut class sizes however as they are not willing to invest the money that would be required. My school is bursting at the seams – we have no breakout space at all. Even the new builds in the area have not got enough classrooms to cut class sizes.

Laura

I would ensure that every Primary School has access to a PE specialist or specialist PE support. Current PE provision is sporadic or sport-led which can alienate pupils. The physical, social and cognitive benefits that quality PE provides should not be underestimated, and these will carry on beyond school. I am the only in school Primary PE teacher in our authority (via PEF funding) and the impact on health & wellbeing and developing positive attitudes to PE and physical activity has been inspiring. This should not be an anomaly in Scottish primary schools; it should be the norm.

Dominic

I would change the top down nature of school management. 'We are doing this.' 'You need to do it this way because document X says so.' There is very little input from actual classroom teachers on these edicts! If Scottish education listened to what teachers actually thought would be a good idea – and just as importantly what is a bad idea – and if they trusted the professionalism and passion of staff instead of treating them like irritations then that would make a massive difference.

Chris

More non-contact time for staff. Since moving overseas in 2015 the difference in terms of contact time has been clear – I now get all my planning, preparation and marking done in school, meaning that time after school in the evenings, at the weekends and in holidays is largely my own. It has made a huge difference to my own wellbeing and I see the same in colleagues who have moved from Scotland – it means that our energy levels are higher and our teaching more focused because we know that, at 4.30, we can leave it all in the classroom until the next day.

Keith

More and regular opportunities for teaching staff to learn from each other, across schools, clusters and contexts (primary and uni). Staff learning and development of skills, knowledge and pedagogy make a huge difference to learning and teaching. This should be led by teachers, not always local authorities.

Kevin

Remove high-stakes SQA exams to make way for mastery-based continuous assessment. This gives pupils and teachers more choice in subject content and allows for curiosity.

Chris

Parents

In response to the difficulties of online learning during the pandemic I'd love to see a legacy of everyone having access to national lessons from a central source so if for whatever reason this happens again no-one is disadvantaged by how good or bad their teachers are at delivering an online syllabus. Those lessons would be available for anyone online and could be accessed 24 hours to work through at their own pace.

Catriona

Education Secretary role at ScotGov should always be an individual with direct teaching/lecturing experience. There are MSPs with this experience – we need teachers, real teachers having a seat at the table in government, and not just through their unions.

Jenny

The introduction of a truly play-based kindergarten stage for 3-7 year olds will allow children to develop naturally and at their own pace in these critical early years. This will also develop their social-emotional skills, resulting in better emotional resilience and mental health throughout their entire lives with no detriment to their academic education. It will also help to close the attainment gaps between socioeconomic groups and gender as far more children are ready for formal education at seven than four.

Steph

More pupil support assistants. I strongly believe that there should be a permanent, full-time PSA in every primary school classroom and probably double the amount that they currently have in secondary schools. This would be a huge support to both teachers and pupils.

Kate

I would incorporate much more free play time into primary schools – there's no need for expensive equipment or specialists or training. Just let the children play. At this present moment in time, as we recover from a year of upheaval and isolation, my children are desperate for play – not supervised, not interfered with, not arranged. They just need time to play with their friends. I know this will help them recover, work through all the emotions and uncertainties they've had to deal with, and in the long run help them to learn more effectively. I wish teachers would get out of the way, stop talking about health and safety, stop trying to get children to play a certain way, stop shortening break times, stop using loss of break time as a punishment, and just let them get on and get outside and play.

Anna

Accountability. The new level system means parents are only given information on progress every couple of years, and report cards are now a copy and paste exercise and tell you nothing. This allows kids, particularly those with ASN to fall behind when parents could be helping them if they knew they were struggling. The lack of information shared equals a lack of accountability to the child.

Susan

More positive contact with parents in areas of social deprivation so they can engage more in their child's education, especially a focus on encouraging fathers or male carers to participate. I noticed at our school it's always the 'middle-class' parents (mums) who lead on things and they tend to be in established cliques which is off putting for other parents. When parents engage more with their kids' education it leads to better outcomes for the child which can improve life at home and connection with the school.

Lynn

As a father of children with additional support needs I concur with the concern of children being 'excluded in the main'. A key issue for ensuring all children can get sufficient tailored attention and support is staff – numbers of teachers and classroom assistants in the classroom (along with small class sizes and ensuring staff receive enhanced, quality, and ongoing training).

A second issue – the elephant in the room – is private schools. Two tiers of education and segregation of children based on ability to pay. Not sure there is the political will to take this on though.

David

Abolish private schools. We have an apartheid school system that structurally disadvantages state school pupils. If everyone went to their local state school, there would be such power behind the other demands that would make a difference: smaller class sizes; more classroom assistants and resources to ensure that the policy of inclusion works; more IT resources etc. because all sectors of society would be asking for them. Some of the challenges faced by teachers in state schools are those caused by wider societal problems, connected to inequality. If everyone was in the same school system, there would be a wider interest in tackling inequalities. We can't improve Scottish schools by only focusing on education policy, so having a wider consensus on tackling inequality through for example more progressive taxation is crucial. We will only get agreement for that from higher taxpayers if their kids are in the state school system.

Claire

Think we require to, in conjunction with teachers, parents and communities, define what a teacher's role is. Are they employed to teach our children core subjects like maths, English etc? Do we as parents and local communities expect them to be ad hoc carers and counsellors, or should other agencies, including parents, step up to their roles? What expectations do we have of external agencies attached to the schools? What expectations should we have of parents?

Lesley Ann

I would change the whole focus of secondary school education from 'passing exams' to 'learning for life'. I don't blame individual teachers or schools but I feel the 'attainment' agenda (measuring schools based on their exam results) has eroded the joy of learning I experienced when I was at school in the 1980s. Perhaps I am reflecting through rose-tinted specs but I feel my two teenagers are being taught 'how to pass exams' instead of being taught to be curious, enquiring and passionate about learning new knowledge and skills.

Lesley

All staff should receive mandatory and comprehensive ASN training. More and more children require additional support and with more training staff would be better placed to identify and respond to individual needs earlier meaning quicker and more positive outcomes for children. With mainstreaming the school environment must be more inclusive and accepting of differing needs than it is now.

Nicole

I would put social workers or link workers or mental health professionals in all schools and ensure a link to community groups, activities and resources. I think children need someone to advocate for their social and community wellbeing as much as their educational attainment. Someone who is there to link children up with activities (for fun!) and who can support families and children and young people to have the support and knowledge about their local community.

Meghan

Greater support for career changers to move into teaching in Scotland, perhaps an Open University qualification for instance. Having worked in schools offering a free service to assist with CfE a decade ago many teachers admitted they at times found it hard to convey the relevance of what was taught. One described their situation as being a pupil, becoming a uni student and then straight back to school as a teacher and so never really having left education at any time. As an electrician I was able to show real-world applications for trigonometry and algebra that I used on a regular basis. I believe there would be real value in more mature individuals having the opportunity to become teachers. I looked into becoming a primary teacher myself about five years ago and there's not a chance I could afford to go through the training unfortunately.

Jack

I'd like to see some of the history of Gaelic and languages in Scotland in general taught to all. Gaelic awareness is important to increase tolerance and encourage learning. And also availability of Gaelic both as a subject and a medium of teaching. At present, most children go through school learning nothing at all about Gaelic and long-standing misconceptions about the language ('they never spoke Gaelic here' etc.) go unchallenged.

Alasdair

Destinations: placing value on a wider range of positive outcomes. College/vocational or entering meaningful work/apprenticeships should be as valued and as supported as pursuing university education. Education should be a lifelong pursuit: people can and should be able to come back to it if they wish or need, including higher education.

Euan

I would like to see a prioritisation of duty to professionalism over duty to employer in the GTCS professional standards. This would enable teachers to freely provide their professional judgement without risking disciplinary action if their view digressed from that of their employer. I believe this would empower teachers to create other necessary changes such as the de-politicisation of education so that policies such as the introduction of a kindergarten stage for 3-7 year olds could be introduced without an education minister worrying about not being able to claim the credit for the impact that would make.

Patricia

Whole family support services linked to school communities can catch many social, emotional and financial issues before they grow and result in more serious harm for children, young people and their parents and carers. Having access embedded in our universal education system can reduce stigma & ensure help is available at the earliest possible point (reducing the need for more intensive support from CAMHS or social work at a later stage), meaning every child or young person comes to school 'ready to learn'.

Maureen

 ## Pupils

From personal experiences I believe that there needs to be more support and education based on trauma and difficult life experiences. I feel as though many of

these things are brushed under the carpet and still a taboo subject but it needs to be normalised. It is unfair that children and teenagers don't get this education as it would be beneficial to so many people as they are expected to carry on with school work like normal.
Abby

The SQA should be completely restructured with the help of teachers. Teachers should be able to have more say over what they are teaching and how they assess their pupils. Obviously it all needs to be regulated and standardised but after the last two years it's clear the SQA is in desperate need of a change.
Eve

A restructuring of the curriculum and re-evaluation of exams as an effective means of assessment (they can be, to an extent, but not for the most part!). I can only speak on behalf of subjects I have studied, however I imagine there are some shared opinions across the board. In Physics, and I extend this to science in general, it all feels very content crammed, with a desperate need to tick outcomes and learn exam technique rather than focusing on the learning of really quite fascinating stuff. Science is a very practical subject, and currently due to the amount of content there is to get through in the 160 hours, its rarely possible to conduct the experiments which I feel really boost understanding. If more time could be allocated then there would be less pressure to get through a course, and attention could be paid to developing understanding, carrying out practical tasks, and developing a deeper knowledge. This time is instead wasted learning how the SQA (very particularly) want things worded in an exam. This may mean reducing the number of subjects studied at Higher so more time can be allocated to each column, but so be it! I think four qualifications where students have a solid understanding of the content rather than how to perform in an exam is preferable to 5 qualifications where answers have been practiced, learned and ready to be recited onto a page.

Jake

No exams. This would mean that teachers weren't teaching to an exam syllabus, and I wouldn't be expected to memorise booklets and booklets of quotes off by heart to parrot back to them. I'd rather have the opportunity to develop proper critical thinking skills and have the opportunity to find things out for myself. That all stopped the minute I started my Nat 5 courses this year and I don't feel as interested or engaged as I used to.

Alex

The curriculum needs to be updated as it is currently teaching us outdated information especially in climate education which is barely in the curriculum at the moment. School should be more nature focused and play to pupils' strengths instead of forcing them to conform and memorise pointless information. I would love to see schools based more outside with a greater focus on current affairs (society and climate/nature).

Anna

Climate Education throughout all subjects (especially core) as currently there is very little of this even if you choose three sciences, geography or modern studies. The world we will grow up into is one that will be heavily impacted and shaped by the climate crisis and we need to be aware and equipped with the tools to tackle this as well as the climate justice side of it.

Leah

Proper mental health support is needed as currently there is very little support for students and at least half of my friends are significantly struggling with the stresses of exams and school life. There needs to be a move away from exams as they benefit certain people and not others, but we also need to be careful not to allow for more racism and homophobia to be present when teacher judgment is relied on.

Esther

We need to teach students transferable skills to face the climate and ecological crisis. The world will not look like it does today so schools must focus on skills that give students access to clean, green jobs and further training or education.

I would also like to see climate justice baked into every subject and course from early ages to build solidarity and responsibility for looking after our planet and communities. This means seeing the climate crisis as not only environmental and physical in nature, although that is important as is basic knowledge of climate science, but as an issue that touches every aspect of society including anti-racism, gender equality and political movements.

I also believe that schools should be more inclusive of gender non-conforming or gender expansive people who do not identify solely as male or female, such as non-binary people. Some steps I would love to see would be to be welcoming of students who use pronouns other than she/he such as they or multiple sets of pronouns. Students who transition to their gender identity should be accepted and free to change their name/pronouns if they wish, and to play on gendered sports teams or access bathrooms that match their identity.

May

Allow students to bring a restricted amount of self-composed notes into each exam, regardless of subject. At present the SQA exams are fixated entirely on the wealth of information that a pupil can maintain for 12 months – little emphasis is placed on the actual real-life skill or application of knowledge required for success in these exams. In most cases you can expect pupils to completely forget the entirety of a course's content once an assessment has been completed, so I feel I would benefit most from learning how to make concise notes of my understanding, refer to relevant sources and apply my own knowledge in the moment, rather than have to memorise a year's worth of learning for a few hours' worth of assessment. I am unsure of where to actually draw the line in the sand for allowed amount/content of the notes (an element of personal understanding must be preserved) but the current system makes me feel as though the SQA are actively trying to prevent learners from demonstrating the full range of their skill and understanding – letting

candidates monitor and perfect these areas through writing notes is, in my view, a step in a fairer direction.
AJ

I would scrap exams. They cause unnecessary stress and other mental health issues and are extremely difficult for neurodivergent people to deal with. I have ADHD, which affects my memory and concentration skills, so exams are a nightmare for me and I can imagine that others have it even worse. They do not gauge how well someone knows a subject, they gauge how well someone can regurgitate some information about that subject. I would replace them with smaller assessments throughout the year and coursework to make the system fairer and accessible for everyone.
Cameron

A complete overhaul of the current curriculum. PSE should include LGBTQ+ people in sex ed, and include things such as financial education to prepare us for leaving school. History should be decolonised to accurately portray the horrors of the British empire and how our country is the way it is because of exploitation and slavery.
Emma

In history we should be taught recent and often overlooked history in Britain such as the Black civil rights movement and British Black Panthers, the movement for LGBT rights and AIDS crisis, working-class movements, Scotland's involvement in colonialism and the slave trade and the history of immigration and immigrant experiences in Scotland (not just pre-

WW2). We should also cover more relevant history like the Iraq war, Chernobyl, deindustrialisation in Britain, devolution and the independence movement, deregulation and privatisation.

Skye

Others

Scottish schools should reintroduce Classics to the curriculum. These subjects boost literacy and provide training in source evaluation, critical comparison, articulating arguments and understanding competing identities. They allow young Scots to think about a whole civilisation in the round, appreciating and analysing society through both literature and art. At present, access to these subjects is largely restricted to learners in the independent sector. This is a matter of social justice which must be remedied. Both Latin and Classical Studies are included as subjects in Curriculum for Excellence and are offered by SQA at all levels. Projects like Advocating Classics Education and Classics in Communities have worked in partnership with the Scotland's National Centre for Languages and Glasgow City Council to make a start, but more must be done if we are to equalise opportunities for all Scottish learners to learn about the ancient world.

Arlene, academic

From an early years perspective we need a kindergarten stage, so no formal schooling until age seven and a requirement rather than guidance for them to be outside for longer periods, every day in all weathers. The natural environment is already understood to be great for children's development, real learning and wellbeing. Then to continue the play element and the outdoor learning for longer as a real choice. Do away with worksheets!

Barbara, childminder

A more inclusive curriculum coupled with teacher CPD.

Brian, community educator

I would move to permanently blended learning so that neurodivergent children can have the experience of being in a class with others but can learn from home when school becomes too much.

Jill, disability activist

Raise school start age to seven and offer a developmentally appropriate curriculum.

Deborah, lecturer

Include training on child development for all new and current teachers. This would create a cultural shift away from tests and academic-led teaching while improving adult knowledge on brain development, attachment and the impact of poverty and trauma. I believe this would make a difference and could lead to more responsive teaching based on the individual child's needs and a realisation of the importance of relationships, improving outcomes and experiences for all children.

Lindsay, early years practitioner

Discipline in schools need an overhaul. It will improve public health and educational outcomes, not just now but for future generations because authoritarian discipline is harming mental health. Too many schools claim to have a nurturing approach yet continue to put children on time out, isolation or suspension. We need an authoritative approach that encompasses empathy and teaching instead of punishment and shame.

Anonymous, early years practitioner

We need to stop having level 6 qualifications as the only measure of success. School is only the beginning of a journey. Teachers should be asked to have more focus on the skills and not just the paper at the end. The idea of skills for work, life and learning should be used to build a curriculum that truly gets it right for every child.

Peter, education worker

The one thing I would change is teacher class contact time. The recent typo in the SNP 2021 Election Manifesto, a reduction of 90 minutes per day, is the sort of step change that is actually required (i.e. a reduction from a maximum of 22.5 hours per week to 15 hours per week). This would bring Scotland in line with countries such as Estonia, Finland, South Korea and Japan. The fact that Scottish teachers have one of the highest class contact times in the world is a major barrier to many other positive developments happening. Teachers do not have the time or space to make real improvements to the quality of education available and the educational outcomes of our young people. However, a reduction in class contact time needs to be matched with effective use of the time freed up. If educational outcomes are to be improved it is essential that teachers focus on improving their classroom practices with a relentless focus on improving teaching and learning. This requires good quality professional learning relevant to the context of the teacher. This sort of change in professional learning, with a move away from wasteful one-off events where there is little coherence or opportunity to revisit, embed, practice, evaluate, develop and improve, will bring real benefits to the quality of teaching and learning and to the morale of teachers with corresponding improvements in teacher retention and professionalism. If such changes are made there can hopefully also be a move away from the stifling external national accountability culture to one of a much more local and internal peer accountability. Perhaps this could genuinely be called teacher empowerment.

Stuart, education manager (and former teacher)

I'd pull together the different technology courses into a coherent curriculum designed around making things / engineering. Techy drawing, CAD, design, woodwork, metalwork to be combined with Digital Computing, IoT, Robotics and then link that as appropriate to the sciences and maths. Essentially combine Techy and Computer Science into an overarching Engineering that sits alongside and complements abstract Science and Maths by connecting them to building things.

Simon, IT industry professional

I would change the school starting age and have a play and relationship based approach when they do.

Smaller class sizes and more staff to support this. Parents, early years, teachers and support staff all working together to give children the best start in life.

Linda, early years worker

Start with love! We need to have love and kindness as the foundation for all we do and then build on this.

Julie, lecturer

An increase in non-contact time to be used for effective professional learning. However teachers need to be seen as professionals so should be free to use this professional learning as they see fit. This time could be used for teachers to read more about teaching and learning strategies for their stage/subject area, observe/share practice with other teachers, read, get involved in curriculum-making etc. This should have a great impact on teachers' knowledge and skills in the classroom.

Colin, lecturer

Interrogatory teaching practices to help critical thinking. STEM students should engage with conflicting sources like humanities/SocSci students do.

George, background unspecified

Moving towards bilingual medium primary schooling. Get a modern language taught as early as possible and introduce some teaching of other things in the second language early on. Kids have to use it to retain it. English-only speakers are at a massive disadvantage in the world and language skills are both harder to acquire in adulthood and less beneficial to the rest of a child's education the later they're developed. As a school pupil I learned more about the English language from French classes and writing essays in History than I feel I ever did in an English class.

Graeme, civil servant

Children starting formal education at seven. I believe this would give them more time to develop language skills, emotional regulation, play, more freedom, more time to develop interests and a love for learning. I truly believe this would help the attainment gap.

Louise, speech and language therapist

I'd like to see the opportunity for Gaelic Medium Education to be available widely across the country, providing parents and carers with a choice of whether they want their child to be educated through either Gaelic or English. To help parents make informed choices, they should be provided with solid, research-based evidence on the advantages of bilingualism-both cognitive and social. Let's have a vision for Scotland where bilingualism and indigenous languages such as Gaelic thrive. Our schools can impact powerfully on how we in Scotland promote respect for cultural diversity through recognising and valuing our Gaelic cultural heritage.

Jim, Stiùiriche Foghlaim (Director of Gaelic Education)

Give every teacher a quality laptop and provide tech support that works for them at home and in school. Before giving learners the technology (which is great) the teachers need it. There should be no expectation of teachers to provide this themselves.

Richard, lecturer

My experience of effective support in schools has been being able to work out of hours (morning and overnight) and in the school to support the underlying causes behind lower attainment in young people from more challenging circumstances. For example, supporting a stressed parent with bedtime and morning routines by supporting them with their mental health, helping a family struggling financially that can't afford a uniform that fits by buying them a few then paying their electricity and wifi bill, or allowing children with specific needs within the school to have those needs met to maximise attendance (e.g. allow an autistic child to arrive late to avoid the crowds, or to wear a non-uniform hat that is comforting). A quick coordinated intervention can do wonders, without necessarily needing a stigmatising referral to Social Work, and potentially avoiding one all together.

Gary, charity worker

Selected Data Sources and Further Reading

Scottish Government data for schools
https://www.gov.scot/collections/school-education-statistics/

Curriculum for Excellence documentation
https://education.gov.scot/education-scotland/scottish-education-system/policy-for-scottish-education/policy-drivers/cfe-building-from-the-statement-appendix-incl-btc1-5/what-is-curriculum-for-excellence

SQA statistics
https://www.sqa.org.uk/sqa/78673.html
Scottish Credit and Qualifications Framework (SCQF):
https://scqf.org.uk/about-the-framework/interactive-framework/

2020 OECD report into Scottish education
https://www.oecd.org/education/scotland-s-curriculum-for-excellence-bf624417-en.htm

Information about the International Council of Education Advisers
https://www.gov.scot/groups/international-council-of-education-advisers

OECD Programme for International Student Assessment (PISA)
https://www.oecd.org/pisa

OECD Education at a Glance 2020
https://www.oecd.org/education/education-at-a-glance

Coalition for Racial Equality and Rights
https://www.crer.scot

Teaching in a Diverse Scotland: increasing and retaining minority ethnic teachers
https://www.gov.scot/publications/teaching-diverse-scotland-increasing-retaining-minority-ethnic-teachers-scotlands-schools

The Promise to Scotland's care experienced young people
https://www.thepromise.scot

The National Centre on Education and the Economy (USA)
https://ncee.org

'Does Teaching Experience Increase Teacher Effectiveness? A Review of the Research', Tara Kini & Anne Podolsky (Learning Policy Institute)
https://learningpolicyinstitute.org/product/does-teaching-experience-increase-teacher-effectiveness-review-research

International Baccalaureate
https://www.ibo.org

'The Leaning Tower of Pisa', Pasi Sahlberg & Andy Hargreaves
https://pasisahlberg.com/the-leaning-tower-of-pisa

What do the PISA results tell us about Scottish education; Prof Mark Priestley and Dr Marina Shapira
https://mrpriestley.wordpress.com/2019/12/06/what-do-the-pisa-results-tell-us-about-scottish-education/

'Teacher quality: why it matters, and how to get more of it', Prof Dylan Wiliam.
https://www.dylanwiliam.org/Dylan_Wiliams_website/Papers_files/Spectator%20talk.doc

The Times Educational Supplement Scotland
https://www.tes.com/news/hub/scotland

Scottish Education, ed Bryce, Humes, Gillies and Kennedy
Edinburgh University Press

Acknowledgements

THIS BOOK HAS been so long in development, but written so quickly, that I really don't know where to start when it comes to acknowledging all the people who helped make it possible.

I suppose it makes sense to begin with the obvious: I wouldn't be doing any of this, or be enjoying the life I currently have, had I not become a teacher. That being the case, there are a few people who need to be thanked personally.

The first is Claire McKeen, one of my oldest, closest, and most honest friends, who long ago told me – in no uncertain terms, and over an indeterminate amount of red wine – that I was only refusing to apply for teaching courses out of stubbornness, having declared after my university graduation that I would, under no circumstances, be heading back to school. She was right about that, and she was also right when she told me to get over myself.

Next is, of course, Alan Kelly, who did so much for me that I'll never really be able to properly thank him. Alan used to say that it was his job to make sure I could do mine: he never asked to see weeks' worth of lesson plans, or reflective journal entries about my classes, because we talked about all of that, and more, every single day. He encouraged me to experiment with the literature and other materials I used in my classes while showing me all the basics, like marking a pile of papers one question at a time, rather than one student at a time, in order to improve consistency. I always felt like he trusted me, and that gave me all the confidence I needed to become (I think) a good teacher.

I also need to thank Marianne Costello, a fantastic chemistry teacher who also studied at UWS, also ticked the box, and had also been sent to Arran as a probationer on a one-year contract. Having realised the cost of rent on the island we decided, after a grand total of maybe half a dozen prior conversations, to live together. We found a flat overlooking Lamlash Bay that was five minutes' walk from the school and – being located directly above it – about 30 seconds away from the pub. It was dangerously convenient and sort of affordable, and aside from the leaky roof, mouldy walls and useless heaters it was a nice place to live. As we were effectively working on temporary contracts my then fiancé (now wife) and I decided it would be best if she didn't move over to the island right away – instead, one of us would visit the other each Friday before returning on the Sunday. We therefore spent most of my first year in teaching apart, and there were plenty of times when that distance, combined with the crushing workload of the first year in the job, just seemed a bit too much. I don't think I've ever told her this, so I'll just put it here and hope that she has bought a copy: I'd never have made it through that year without Marianne's help and friendship.

There are others who made my time at Arran High School so special and, in all sorts of ways, helped bring me to where I am now: colleagues (and friends) like Brian Donlin, Amanda Hogge, Heather Johnstone, David Fyfe, Matt Reid, Sarajane Moffat, Heather Gough and many more, as well as so many pupils who, I hope they know, meant the world to me. The only thing I would change is that it ended far too soon.

But this book wouldn't have happened unless two distinct strands in my life came together. The first is my experience in teaching, but the second is my emerging role as a journalist specialising in Scottish education. That all started thanks to Angela Haggerty (formerly editor of CommonSpace) who gave me the early support and opportunities that made subsequent successes possible. I am also forever in the debt of Rob Edwards, who taught me a great deal about the FOI laws that would go on to underpin so much of my work, and Jamie Maxwell, whom I first met during the 2016 election campaign (I was a list candidate for a small, left-wing and entirely unsuccessful party called RISE and he was brought in as the press officer) and whose support and encouragement has been invaluable over the years.

I would also like to thank the various editors and publishers who allowed me to explore and write about other interests. I have been lucky enough to cover issues such as Arran's housing crisis, Bernie Sanders' 2016 primary campaign in New York City, the recovery from devastating forest fires on La Gomera, and even the pro-independence, anti-government demonstrations in Catalonia in 2019, all of which has been useful preparation for the process of writing this book.

I am of course extremely grateful to all of the other people – from teachers and leading education experts to friends and acquaintances – who helped me to get this far, whether that meant reading early drafts and sample chapters, suggesting improvements, offering encouragement or, for many of them, simply listening to my no doubt endless rants about the problems in schools over the years. A special mention is also necessary for Ali and Dino Wright, owners of the quite wonderful Dunans Cottage in Knapdale where I spent a fantastic long weekend finishing my first full draft of the book, and my mum, who let me turn her dining room into a temporary office when I needed somewhere else to work. And of course, none of this would be possible without the assistance and dedication of everyone at Luath Press.

Most of all, however, I want to thank my wife, Ruth, and my son, Ciaran, without whom I would simply be lost.

Ruth and I have been together since we were teenagers, and next year will be our ten-year wedding anniversary. We've been through plenty in that time, from house moves and health scares to that time a glass of red wine *somehow* ended up all over her face and nobody was to blame at all, but she has always been endlessly supportive of the work that I do and the way I go about it. She is the best, bravest person I have ever met and knowing that she believes in me always makes it a good deal easier to believe in myself. To be frank, she's way out of my league, and I don't know what I'd do without her.

And then there is Ciaran, who turned seven while I was writing this book, his second birthday of the coronavirus era. He is going into primary three at a fantastic nearby school where his favourite things are football, gardening, maths and the day when they get cheesy pasta for lunch. He's far too young to understand this, but just knowing that he is around always makes everything a little brighter; sometimes when you're struggling through a 60,000-odd word manuscript what you really need is your kid to pop their head around the door just to see how you're getting on. Ciaran also had a habit of coming into my office and reading whatever page I had up on the screen, and on several occasions helped me identify and correct some mistakes. He even typed up some of my handwritten corrections as I read them aloud from a printed draft. By my reckoning, making such a tangible contribution to a real book must cover a good selection of the relevant Experiences and Outcomes for his age and stage.

Finally, I want to mention the teachers, parents and pupils who have shared their stories with me over the last five years. This book, like all of my reporting before it, has always been about trying to get to the truth of Scottish education – but even if the available data were completely reliable, it could still only ever offer a limited picture of the day-to-day realities in classrooms (and staffrooms) across Scotland. Everyone who has ever come to me to raise a concern, nudge me towards a developing problem, ask for advice or even just share their experience has contributed to this book more than they will ever know. I hope I have done your stories justice.

Thank you all.

Luath Press Limited

committed to publishing well written books worth reading

LUATH PRESS takes its name from Robert Burns, whose little collie Luath (*Gael.*, swift or nimble) tripped up Jean Armour at a wedding and gave him the chance to speak to the woman who was to be his wife and the abiding love of his life. Burns called one of the 'Twa Dogs' Luath after Cuchullin's hunting dog in Ossian's *Fingal*. Luath Press was established in 1981 in the heart of Burns country, and is now based a few steps up the road from Burns' first lodgings on Edinburgh's Royal Mile. Luath offers you distinctive writing with a hint of unexpected pleasures.

Most bookshops in the UK, the US, Canada, Australia, New Zealand and parts of Europe, either carry our books in stock or can order them for you. To order direct from us, please send a £sterling cheque, postal order, international money order or your credit card details (number, address of cardholder and expiry date) to us at the address below. Please add post and packing as follows: UK – £1.00 per delivery address; overseas surface mail – £2.50 per delivery address; overseas airmail – £3.50 for the first book to each delivery address, plus £1.00 for each additional book by airmail to the same address. If your order is a gift, we will happily enclose your card or message at no extra charge.

Luath Press Limited
543/2 Castlehill
The Royal Mile
Edinburgh EH1 2ND
Scotland
Telephone: +44 (0)131 225 4326 (24 hours)
Email: sales@luath.co.uk
Website: www.luath.co.uk